NETWORKING in 90 MINUTES

For a complete list of Management Books 2000 titles,
visit our web-site on http://www.mb2000.com

The original idea for the 'In Ninety Minutes' series was
presented to the publishers by Graham Willmott, author
of 'Forget Debt in Ninety Minutes'. Thanks are due to
him for suggesting what has become a major series to
help business people, entrepreneurs, managers,
supervisors and others to greatly improve their personal
performance, after just a short period of study.

Other titles in the 'in Ninety Minutes' series are:

Forget Debt in 90 Minutes
Understand Accounts in 90 Minutes
Working Together in 90 Minutes
25 Management Techniques in 90 Minutes
Supply Chain in 90 Minutes
Practical Negotiating in 90 Minutes
Faster Promotion in 90 Minutes
Find That Job in 90 Minutes
Become a Meeting Anarchist in 90 Minutes
Telling People in 90 Minutes
Strengths Coaching in 90 Minutes
Perfect CVs in 90 Minutes
Budgeting in 90 Minutes
Payroll in 90 Minutes
... other titles will be added

The series editor is James Alexander

Submissions of possible titles for this series or for management
books in general will be welcome. MB2000 are always keen to
discuss possible new works that might be added to their extensive
list of books for people who mean business.

Networking to Improve Your Netw£rk!

NETWORKING
in 90
Minutes

Lindsay Bannerman

Cartoons by Stephen Cuffe of www.imagesinbusiness.com

2000

First published in 2006 by Management Books 2000 Ltd
Forge House, Limes Road
Kemble, Cirencester
Gloucestershire, GL7 6AD, UK
Tel: 0044 (0) 1285 771441
Fax: 0044 (0) 1285 771055
E-mail: info@mb2000.com
Web: www.mb2000.com

Printed and bound in Great Britain by Digital Books Logistics Ltd of Peterborough

British Library Cataloguing in Publication Data is available

ISBN 1-85252-479-0

Contents

About the Author

Lindsay Bannerman is one of the UK's leading networking experts. She was named as one of Scotland's Top 100 Influential Business Women within 16 months of starting her own business. Regularly invited as keynote speaker to many business audiences, Lindsay's growing network of colleagues and contacts refer to her as the 'Networking Queen' and with a wealth of experience and a multi-award winning company to prove it, she has a lot to say on the subject of successful networking.

See www.networkingin90mins.com

Introduction

Why a book on Networking? A feature of the age we live in is the realisation that there are lots of different ways of improving your life.

People join gymnasiums and health clubs, take up running, cut back on caffeine and hire life coaches. They read self-improvement manuals, get colour tests to make sure they are wearing the right coloured clothes, and scan the astrology charts for a sign that good things are just round the corner.

Yet the communication skills we learn as we develop into adulthood are often ignored or taken for granted. This book is a rule-of-thumb guide to tapping into those skills and exploiting them in our personal and business lives, not only for career advancement but for the satisfaction and security that a growing network of friends and colleagues bring.

In a step-by-step progression, I will show how simple it is to meet people, give a good impression of yourself and your company or product, increase your circle of friends and business acquaintances, and help others along the way. I will discuss how to be remembered along with your service or product and get others talking for you. How to keep in touch and maintain your contacts without pestering.

With a wealth of experience and a multi-award winning company to prove it, I have a lot to say on the subject.

'All our knowledge has its origins in our perceptions.'
Leonardo da Vinci

Life's not fair

If it were then the most talented and highly qualified people would be at the top and it would be a natural progression in moving up the ladder. Perhaps you think it works like that and therefore networking is a waste of time? This book is not for you.

Sometimes people just land on their feet and the clients, the contracts, the job promotions, and new job opportunities line up at the door. This book might not be for that person.

Yet there are lots of businesses all around you who need products, services, staff, ideas and materials – businesses which decide to award these procurements, contracts, promotions, pitches and orders based on who comes first in an alphabetical flick through the Yellow Pages, simply because they don't know you are there.

A multi-million pound advertising campaign is one way round the problem, another is to spend 90 minutes learning the secrets of networking. If that is you, clutch this book tightly in two hands and with a firm and steady gait, walk to the cashier and change your life!

Networking, put simply, is meeting people, chatting, learning about them and telling them about you. The more you do it, the wider and more useful your personal network. You learn who has strengths in particular areas, who is reliable, cost effective (to their face, cheap behind their back) and a whole lot of people know who you are, and what you can do for them.

This book sets out a series of tried and trusted techniques to tap into the networks buzzing around you. With practical examples and the

> 'Everything happens to everybody sooner or later
> if there is time enough.'
>> George Bernard Shaw

experience of a Professional Networker, it will take you through a variety of ways to improve your visibility and that of your product or service or professional skill, and hopefully have some fun along the way.

'Success is how high you bounce when you hit bottom.'
General George Patton

1

First Thoughts

Have you ever learned to network? Have you ever learned a foreign language? Any foreign language course will usually start by reassuring you that you already know a lot of the words (Okay, not if you are learning Mandarin, but work with me here) and you are a lot further down the path of learning than you realised.

There are two bits of good news with regards to learning how to network.

1. You already know how to network ... and
2. you don't need to learn a foreign language to do it.

In fact you learned to network from a very early age, so think of this as a refresher course.

We have all been at schools where we had to mingle with people we didn't know, new jobs where we wanted to know and be known by our colleagues, job interviews, first dates, parties and just about any social event you care to mention. I am not saying that we handled all those situations with a suave self-assurance and ingratiated ourselves in to the hearts of everyone that came across our paths, but it's all experience and as someone once said, we only learn from our mistakes.

> *'Success is the ability to go from one failure to another with no loss of enthusiasm.'*
> Winston Churchill

The aim of this book is to show you how to harness that experience in a way that will enrich your life and your career. If that sounds like a lot to get in the next 90 minutes of reading, then think about what you want to achieve here: you know who you are, your strengths and weaknesses. You probably know what you want in the future and deep down have a pretty good idea how to get it. But just as you found yourself a little tongue tied when you first arrived at the gates of a new school with your blazer still itchy and the unfamiliar feel of a new school tie knotted around your neck, there is the danger of blowing it when you come face to face with a potential new client, or boss or career opportunity. It helps to have a few notes discreetly scribbled on the inside of your cuff – how else would you have passed that chemistry exam in 4th year?

You!

Another thing to bear in mind here, is that it is yourself you are selling and that is a subject that you are uniquely qualified to do. This book will simply show you how to organise yourself and your thoughts; ensure that you don't have that rotten feeling where you suddenly remember an hour later the thing you could have said. The thing that would have made you stand out from the crowd and got you that contract or job or, at the very least, made you memorable the next time the person you met was in a position to help you.

As I hope to show you here, networking is a long-term strategy that continues to reward you for years to come, while the network grows and your contacts with it. You are going to use this device to expand your horizons and increase your friends and colleagues and with it your life. Because you are ultimately the product, the service or merchandise you are selling is inextricably linked with you.

'Creativity is a natural extension of our enthusiasm.'
Earl Nightingale

So throw yourself in to these pages with a carefree abandon and you will come out the other side primed to change your life and your career with the answers at the tip of your tongue, or at the very least at your fingertips, with a Rolodex® bursting with addresses of people who will answer them for you.

One last thing before we start – this is fun! It's legal too (I'm assured the two aren't mutually exclusive) and the more involved you get in serious networking the more fun you will have.

A lot of these events involve champagne that someone else is paying for (says she like a true Scotswoman), and they are usually situations where people are at their happy, enthusiastic best, wanting you to think well of them. You want to make friends and meet people that will be not only be delighted to see you but to invite you along to the next event too. And you will get a kick out of it too – the feeling of getting somewhere, success, promotion and even just having more entries in your address book.

Personal progress

And it gets easier too. Not just with the practice that you will have as you proceed, or being able to remember the formulae without resorting to permanent markers and shirt cuffs, but because of the snowball effect. If all this makes networking sound pretentious and insincere, I apologise because it really shouldn't. Small talk may be dull but we all do it, or should. There is nothing cynical or calculating about putting people at their ease by chatting about the weather or the latest developments in Coronation Street. Far better to have a conversation starter than to stand at the fringe of a group looking gormless.

This isn't about manipulating people or falsely selling yourself – it's

> 'Experience is a hard teacher because she gives the test first, the lesson afterward.'
> Vernon Law

about ensuring you show yourself in the best possible light. Think of it as swotting up before a big exam – if you didn't attend the classes it won't do you much good, but it is reassuring to have the bits and pieces fresh in your memory before you start.

I'm not going to suggest exactly what you say any more than I would tell you how to dress. I want to give you a framework that you can adapt to your own style and needs. Besides, imagine the confusion if everyone at your next networking event also read this book and started quoting it verbatim?

If you let this work for you it will do so by **unlocking** your potential and personality not by replacing them with a set of clichés and glib one-liners.

As your own personal network expands, it will give you access to the networks of the people you meet. This isn't all about you, it's also about being able to help others when they need something you can't personally provide.

As we will discuss, this is one of the most important aspects of Networking. Your phone will stay very quiet if the people you meet think you are going to frantically sell them something every time they ring.

We want to be the hub, the person people phone when they need to find someone with a peculiar skill or service, but we also want to know others with their own resources, if only to shout on them when we come up with a blank when asked if we know a Peruvian Nose Flautist who does Bar Mitzvahs. And no, before you ask I don't know one, but I'm sure I know someone who does…

> 'Man's mind, stretched by a new idea, never goes back to its original dimensions.'
>
> Oliver Wendell Holmes

What is Networking?

Networking is meeting people, and exchanging information. This is something you have been doing since you were in your pram with a bewildering series of strangers forcing their way in to your personal space and saying goo goo goo. So you already have all the experience you need. Except you are probably a little less cute and now have the ability to speak back. Strangely the latter may well reduce the effectiveness of your social interaction if you say the wrong thing when you open your mouth.

Consider that in those early exchanges, you were seen as charming, intelligent (for your age) and left the people you met with a warm feeling, and all you had to do was smile and not throw up in their face (we will get back to that when we move on to 'champagne receptions').

In business, we simply do the same thing – meet people, make friends, and hope they will remember us and what we do if or when they are in the market for our products or services, or just as importantly, know of someone else in that position.

So for the purposes of this book, Networking is marketing yourself or your business or your career using your social skills.

Networking – Room 101?

Every successful concept becomes a cliché sooner or later, and it's the nature of the press and of people in general to doubt that something works or is 'for them' when they think it is has been done and is 'old hat'. The concept of networking is therefore instantly consigned to Room 101. It's a bit like a rock band that someone saw

> 'There are no such things as limits to growth, because there are no limits to the human capacity for intelligence, imagination, and wonder.'
> Ronald Reagan

before they were famous, and as soon as they make it to Top of the Pops, the inevitable, 'Oh, I preferred their early stuff,' comments arise. It doesn't matter what you call it or to what extent it is being doubted as an effective business tool – we will always network and those that are good at it will always have the edge over their competitors who do it badly.

It's an over-used term but an under-used strategy and although it's something that we have a natural ability to do, it's amazing how rarely people consider refining those basic skills or at the very least tweaking them a little. Perhaps it seems calculating and contrived to go in to a meeting with a plan of action, to know what you are going to talk about and what you aim to 'get out' of that gathering. Some people would feel it unsporting to have a prepared speech or a small brochure in their wallet, handbag or sporran.

This seems a shame, because, should you be speaking to someone that just happens to have a multi-zillion pound commission to hand out and you have no pen, business card or leaflet and are feeling a little tongue-tied, you will have to wait to read about it in the papers to find out which of your competitors did get the work. I have never known anyone to be offended by being handed a business card and they often look relieved as they had forgotten your name when you were first introduced.

Networking agenda/objectives

Equally, and for the same reason, it's no bad thing to have a clear idea of what you want before you step in to a room with potential clients. Let's face it – you don't have to step into a room, you can bump in to someone in the street or stuck behind the queue for

> 'We see our customers as invited guests to a party, and we are the hosts. It's our job every day to make every important aspect of the customer experience a little bit better.'   Jeff Bezos

pensions in your local post office. So be clear in your own mind what your priorities are for selling yourself and your business.

What would you say right now if I introduced you to the person who could make all your business dreams come true? Can you name some of your best clients and relate an example of why they use you rather than a competitor? Can you clearly and concisely and using appropriate language for your audience, describe what you do and why you are so good at it? Anything?

Imagine how many times you have already met people with the potential to transform your life, and didn't know it because you didn't say the right thing, or say anything at all. How many people will you meet this month even for a few minutes, who don't know all the services or products that you have to offer.

And if you don't know what you want to sell and what you want to get, how can you expect someone you meet to offer it, or recognise that what they have to offer is what you want?

Networking is the new marketing

Of course, in some ways, networking is the original marketing, but just as our ancestors ran long before we jogged, we wouldn't consider a loin cloth and a club the appropriate accessories in today's world. Yet how many times have you heard someone say that the best form of marketing is a personal referral? Word of mouth?

We live in a world that is suspicious of advertising telling them they can have softer hands if they change their dishwashing liquid for another brand or have safer sex by using their condoms, or that such and such a beer will make you more attractive to the opposite sex.

> 'Your most unhappy customers are your greatest source of learning.'
> Bill Gates

17

But we will still believe a colleague who tells us they know a good plumber when they have a leaking pipe. The Yellow Pages has its place, but 'You've tried the rest now try the best' has been used before. Honest. And you can keep your fingers crossed and hope your friends and acquaintances remember to mention your name, service or whatever it is you are selling, and know just the right thing to say.

Or you can take steps to make sure. It doesn't really matter what you call it or what new buzzwords are added, networking will always be with us in one form or another and there will always be those who ignore it and others exploiting it to the full.

Definition of 'Networking'

Networking is not about manipulating other people. Networking is a simple process of teaching and learning. Networking is about meeting people and exchanging information. Networking is about paying it forward and reaping the success of helping others to help you.

There are eight steps to successful networking:

- unaware to aware
  - aware to curious
    - curious to interested
      - interested to wanting
        - wanting to buying
          - buying to satisfied
            - and the satisfied to the …
              - creation of a **raving** fan!

But we will talk about this later.

> 'Enthusiasm is a vital element toward the individual success of every man or woman.'
>
> Conrad Hilton

Of course, it's not all champagne and canapes. One of the problems with such a generic term is the tendency to dismiss it as something that is not applicable to your personal situation.

I would like to address that problem now. If you have already reached the top of your chosen profession or are making so much money that you really can't be bothered making more, you are correct, networking is not much use to you.

But if networking is a catch-all term, let's look at some sub-divisions.

External networking
This is what most people think of as networking and more like the aforementioned cocktail hour mingling. But that doesn't mean you should dismiss it out of hand.

Remember that you are casting a wide net, and if you go to a reception where no one has any use for your service or product, it's unlikely that there is no one there who has no use for the services and or products of one of your circle of co-networkers. In some ways, that might even be a more fruitful occasion simply because no one will feel pressured when talking to you or assume you are only there to twist their arms up their backs. Apparently this does sometimes happen at Masonic meetings but it's all part of some arcane ritual and doesn't really count and you are fine if you avoid men with one wrinkly trouser leg.

But imagine how much easier it is to extol the virtues of someone you know and whose work you can recommend, than selling yourself? For a start, you don't have that fine balance to find – confident but not brash, enthusiastic about your work without overselling. The idea that what comes around goes around is what really matters here.

> 'Success seems to be connected with action. Successful people keep moving. They make mistakes, but they don't quit.'
> Conrad Hilton

19

The opportunity to talk in a gathering about other people and barely mention yourself is the essence of what we are talking about in this book. You even get to feel good about knowing that you are doing a favour for a friend. When you are successful and you have passed on a fellow networker's name to someone who is interested in meeting them, you find yourself in a win-win situation.

On the one hand, you have potentially solved a problem for the new contact you have just made and saved them the task of tracking down that specialist or nanny or dog walker and they will remember and be grateful if your advice is good.

On the other hand, you can phone the person whose name you pushed (in most cases this can wait until the following day, people tend not to want to hear about it as you stagger out of yet another champagne reception) and tell them the good news. You get to chat with them, give them a 'heads-up' about the phone call they are about to get from a potential new client or employer, and reading between those lines they realise that you spent some of your own time talking about them and trying to get them new work. If they are not tremendously grateful and from that moment on looking for an opportunity to repay the favour, I would be very surprised.

Internal Networking

Who knows you in your own organisation? What impression do your senior managers have of you? Do they know your name? What do you do for them? Who knows how to find that procurement procedure? Who can fast track an order when the client has a sudden emergency? What is the name of the sixteen-year old new starter from registry who delivers the mail? Are you the type of person that no one wants to approach with a problem because you don't invite

> 'To succeed in business, it is necessary to make others see things as you see them.'
>
> Aristotle Onassis

conversation? What is the name of the receptionist where you work and what does she think of you? Think about it.

It's too easy to work hard at impressing your immediate boss and make sure that your reports are in on time and the lapels on your suit jacket are neatly pressed, and in lots of cases these things are noted. But if you ignore everyone else, take no active part in office discussions about who's hot in Emmerdale (it's not important to actually keep up to date with every soap opera or reality tv show, just take the time to know what everyone around you is interested in because it's too easy to sneer at pop culture) then you will find yourself being ignored and on the outside. This is the opposite of the effect your aiming for, a kind of anti-networking.

As with so much of what we are doing here, this all needs to be done in a balanced and natural way. Show an interest in all the people around you, those above you on the corporate ladder and those working alongside you, and make sure that those below you are not overlooked. As for balance, don't spend the whole day around the water cooler collecting gossip – it pays to do some work now and then too! It's all too easy to underestimate the value of 'noticing' the people around you and knowing their names.

Think how pleased you were yourself when a senior manager or partner knew your name and took the time to smile and say 'hi' as she passed you in the corridor. Don't ever make the mistake of being friendly and chatty to the people who work around you and clean the office when you are alone and have loads of time, and then ignore them if you happen to be with a senior member of staff or have a lot on your mind. It's not a good enough excuse – and more importantly you will gain a reputation for being insincere and friendly only when it suits you.

> *'The secret of business is to know something that nobody else knows.'*
> Aristotle Onassis

I watched a perfect example of this a couple of months back when I was visiting a multi-million pound, family-run shop-fitting company. Sitting with some people in the staff canteen, I saw the managing director come in and raised my head to say hello thinking he was coming over to pass the time of day – something this particular director never fails to do – only to realise he hadn't seen me and was zeroing in on a young joiner sitting nearby. I won't name the company or the director as I feel it would betray a confidence, but the conversation went something like this:

Boss   'Hi, I'm sorry, but was it yourself that was in the gym with me last night? *(They had recently fitted out a new gym for the staff)*

Worker   'Yes'

Boss   'I just wanted to apologise; once I get into my routine, I just don't even see people around me and I realised later that it was really rude.'

Worker *(now smiling)* 'No, it's fine.'

Boss   'I also wanted to say that I think you should hold your stretches a little longer in your warm-ups, you might find it helps you from getting stiff ...'

Not only did this person apologise to one of his staff, but he did it at the first opportunity regardless of who was there to hear the apology, and then went on to show interest in the person and offer his advice.

There are very few people with that kind of natural grasp of communications but it won't surprise you to know that the company is full of happy, hard working staff and is always a pleasant place to visit.

'After a certain point, money is meaningless. It ceases to be the goal. The game is what counts.'

Aristotle Onassis

So remember that internal networking should be applied to those below you on the corporate ladder as well as those above.

Career Networking
Similar to Internal Networking but with a broader aspect, career networking is an important strategy for many. Hopefully you have addressed the issues of making yourself known around your own office as we have just discussed, so now it's time to expand on this and make yourself known throughout your organisation and in related companies.

Make a point of attending events that relate to your skills and job prospects. Make yourself known to people who do similar work to yourself with different companies – who knows when they might hear of an opportunity in another organisation, or tell someone else about you, which is even better? Although a lot of what we discuss here is about improving your image and profile, it's always more effective if someone without a vested interest supplies the testimonial.

It's a fact that a lot of jobs are not advertised – but that does not mean you can't be the one who fills the position. A good network will make you aware of positions that are likely to appear and give you time to get talking to the decision makers. Often the person leaving the post will be the ideal source of knowledge and be able to give you a clear idea of the good and bad aspects of the job.

By keeping the network buzzing, you can establish when and where a job might appear; a company which is doing well and expanding or moving in to a new sector might be keen to talk to potential employees or to know who has the experience or expertise or even qualifications to fill a post. In a situation like this, they will be happy to know that they can be up and running in as short a time as possible

> 'You can never quit. Winners never quit, and quitters never win.'
> Ted Turner

23

and not have to wait for two or three months of interviewing and waiting for people to become available.

Remember you are casting a wide net – the wider it's spread, the more chances it will create. Of course you are not attending every event giving the impression that you are desperate for a new job. On the contrary, you will be putting forward the image of someone who is in control, enjoying what they are doing and doing it well and within their ability.

There is nothing more likely to improve your prospects than being 'head-hunted' and if someone knows you are desperate to get out of your current position, they will also assume they can get you cheap. If they are turning up at your door and want to entice you away from a good position they will have to offer more and make it as attractive as possible. So be careful what signals you are putting out – make sure they are positive ones but perhaps avoid saying that you are so happy that nothing and no one will ever get you to change your job!

The same rules apply with multi-national companies, you must make an effort to get to know colleagues in different cities and countries and hemispheres. When there is a visit from some other satellite of your company, do you take the time to make that visitor welcome? Do you know anything about their culture if they come from far away? Surely it's not too difficult to find out if there are special dietary needs or preferences that might be accommodated for instance. And one of the beauties of the society we live in is the ability to keep in touch by email. (I have a friend in Scotland who is in the middle of an online game of chess with someone in India – the time differences mean that the moves are often made on different days, but it is very easy to find common ground no matter what physical or cultural differences exist.)

> *'Don't be afraid to give up the good to go for the great.'*
> John D. Rockefeller

Common ground

This brings us to another point; what do you know about the interest of those around you and what they do when they are not working, with the corollary being – what do they know about you? Finding common ground and showing an interest in each other as unique people is the essence of networking. But you must also give others a chance to know you.

Like any other strategy, it must never be obvious or so contrived that you seem shallow. It will flatter a lot of people for you to look intently in their eyes and with deep sincerity and humility ask them how their pet pekinese is getting on with its new dog food. And then have a follow up question about kennelling in the area and move on to flea powder and ... but you get the point, find ways to get to know people and for them to know you. Don't simply research what they like and then beat them over the head with it.

It's hard to let others know about you without seeming boastful, but if someone asks you what you did at the weekend, then feel free to tell them about the bungee jumping/paragliding. It's just as important to give people an excuse to talk to you as it is for you to find common ground with those around you. If you are the type of person who likes to keep their personal life separate from their professional life, there are still ways of finding common ground.

Just be careful that you are not asking a lot of questions about someone else's life but refusing to divulge any details of your own. Where you are working closely with members of the opposite sex, it is always worth making sure you make it clear that you are as interested in everyone's welfare and not flirting. This is a minefield in its own right but a little common sense and making sure you ask

---

'What separates the winners from the losers is how a person reacts to each new twist of fate.'
Donald Trump

25

appropriate questions and subtle observations will avoid the mines. We all know the man in every office whose only comments on the girls in the office is to mention the shortness of their skirts – don't make that mistake. Once you get the reputation as the office lech or slapper it will stick. I guess if you are the office slapper you might consider it good networking, but that's for another book.

'As long as you're going to be thinking anyway, think big.'
Donald Trump

Networking as a tool for growth

Another important area of networking is growing businesses and those who need to find new markets and new clients and find ways to expand their core business. Networking can not only help but can be a strong solution to these issues.

Businesses are just people in a structure. No matter what happens in the way of business processes and corporate directives, jobs and contracts will always be distributed on the basis of who knows who. It's said that 80% of business contracts come about as a result of networking as well as 90% of jobs. I wonder what percentage of the best contracts and the best jobs go to the best networkers? What is certain is that by being out there and known, you give yourself a chance that might not have existed were you to opt for keeping your head down.

We all know statistics can be manipulated but there is nothing to stop you doing your own. How many people do you know? (Have a look at the address book in your email system for a start) 200? 250? So now imagine that all those people probably know a similar number. That means you are only two steps away from 10,000 people! Pick all the holes you want in these figures but you can't escape the fact you can reach an awful lot of people and percentage-wise there will be a lot of opportunity there.

So for the sake of humouring me, consider that with this as a working hypothesis, every time you make a real and useful contact, it means that your network just increased by 500 people. We will talk further about this subject further on in the book.

But there are other types of growth that are equally valid. You are reading this book because you want to increase your skills, so you

> 'Bear in mind that you almost certainly know more about yourself than anyone else, in spite of any claims they may make.'
> James Alexander

don't need to be sold on the merits of personal growth, life long learning or what ever you want to call it. We all have areas where we can learn and expand our skills and knowledge, and as we do, it inevitably leads to more ways to reach others and make new friends. But acknowledging that there are things we don't know and seeking out those that can help us is another tenet of networking. You never need know how to do something as long as you know someone who does. Of course you may simply want to know for your own sake, so why not ask for help? Most people will be happy to share their skills and be flattered that you came to them in the first place.

The more you look at networking as a way to manage your career or your opportunities, the more it is clear how it touches every aspect of your life, and for the better if you let it. Your company has a squash court in the basement – you can get fit, get to know your colleagues in a social context, have something to talk about when you get back to the office and an excuse to meet up for a comissatory drink later.

Someone is collecting for charity – perhaps you have some spare time at the weekend to help them organise or coordinate their efforts or you know a graphic designer that could do them a cheap flyer. You get to feel good about yourself, help a worthy cause and you make friends with someone else. There are so many opportunities to reach out to those around you. You don't need to take them all, but you might surprise yourself at what extra energy you can generate with the right motivation.

This is a topic I keep returning to: don't always think business when you think networking, instead think 'people' and that helping others and getting involved in leisure pursuits can not only make your life more fulfilling, it can be by far the most effective form of networking.

> 'A brand for a company is like a reputation for a person. You earn reputation by trying to do hard things well.'
>
> Jeff Bezos

2

Why Network?

So, why Network? Perhaps that's obvious now that we have reached chapter two, but sometimes it helps to have clear objectives and be sure in your own mind what you want to achieve.

- You can make **'new friends'** – number one on the list and justly so. You can't be a networker without being sociable, which is tough to achieve if you have no friends!

- **'Meet new people'** in general; have you ever noticed how much your life can change every time there is some new element added to the mix? And surely change is what we are looking at here- that and the desire to make our work and lives more interesting.

- **'Find a new career'**. You might be happy with the one you have, but then again what if there is something out there even better and you don't know about it simply because you don't know the right people.

Add these together, or combine the three, and it leads to so many other possibilities; you want to find a new goalie for your company football team, new buyers for your product, or you might be looking for a new member of your team, or someone with some other special skills.

> *'The future is here. It's just not widely distributed yet.'*
> William Gibson

As ever with this philosophy, the possibilities keep expanding exponentially; with all these new contacts, employees, friends and goalkeepers, you have the potential for new ideas, new working practices, ways to save money, streamline processes, motivate staff, energise your team and so much more.

Never forget that this must always be a two-way street for you to be an effective networking operative; keep listening to those you meet and look at ways of helping them or notice if they might have something of use to an existing contact or friend. And this is not a selfless exercise in philanthropy because the relevant parties will always be grateful for your input and help, and will be even more likely to keep their eyes and ears open for the chance to repay your kindness. Of course, if you recommend a goalkeeper who subsequently lets in three sitters in a row, you may want to change your name and move abroad. Never say I don't offer you alternatives.

Formula for success

I mentioned the idea of having clear objectives for what you want to achieve, another useful tool can be simple rules-of-thumb. Have a look at the people you most admire in business- your own business or perhaps an iconic entrepreneur. There is one thing you can almost guarantee- they will have worked for their position and success. If they had it handed to them on a plate they wouldn't command the same respect, or have any lessons to teach. Another thing they will often have is a mental clarity of vision and goal and I would like to touch on that here.

First let's look at a formula for success:

> *'The empires of the future are the empires of the mind.'*
> Sir Winston Churchill

Ability x Application x Attitude = Achievement

I would suggest that the least important part of this formula is '*ability*' and '*application*' the most important. These are in your own hands, one the result of natural talent and the path (personal or career or education) that led to where you are now, the other the amount of work you are prepared to do in an effort to achieve those goals. Then we have '*attitude*', that is why you are holding this book to your heart. If you didn't value the merits of 'attitude' you would not be looking to refine the way you work or think in the first place. And because it is the part of this formula for success which you can most influence, this book is just one of the tools you can employ to bring about that effect, described by Nigel Risner (motivational speaker) as 'shelf education'.

You probably have a clear idea of your own ability (something which will be affected by your own personality and be a true and objective assessment or not, but for this rule-of-thumb guide, sufficient), and only you will truly know how hard you work and what percentage of this effort is focussed and effective.

So try writing it down, look at it before you start work in the morning and score yourself when you stop for the day. Do that for two weeks and you will easily see where there is room for improvement and be able to concentrate your efforts to improve.

think / plan / do = conceive / plan / deliver

At this point, I feel obliged to you, dear reader, to suggest you don't leave a chart lying around your desk at work that says 'Tuesday, couldn't be arsed – nursing a hangover.' Just a thought.

Here's another device for moving forward in your aims; work

'The best way to predict the future is to invent it.'
Alan Kay

31

backwards. '!?TAHW' I hear you say. What I mean is, imagine you have already achieved your goals, and you are now sitting in the managing director's chair, a deck chair in Barbados, or perhaps handing over a quarterly report to your area manager. Whatever it is, think of it as a concrete reality, and now go into reverse – what would you have done last? What stages might have led to the successful conclusion? Imagine possible hurdles and try to think of how they could be avoided. It's surprising just how much you can see with a different perspective.

Let me demonstrate; take a blank piece of paper and draw a horse. Don't worry about the quality of your penmanship. Now look closely at the sketch and decide what you like about it and what could be improved on. Assess the composition and even the shape. Now hold it up to a mirror (or reverse it and hold it up to a light if you don't have a mirror to hand). Do you see how completely different it looks? It might not look any better (nobody knows how to draw horses, apart from George Stubbs) but I bet it doesn't look like the same drawing. And that is what we are trying to do with the mindset of achieving your dreams. From a different direction and new perspective, perhaps the path you follow is not exactly the one you thought you were on.

With this in mind, perhaps you might want to 'style' yourself to achieve this end. You might not look like the person sitting on one of those chairs in this vision, so what might you look like? What type of person should you be? Now, let's apply this to networking; do others see you as the right person to be sitting in the director's seat? What must you change to be that person? Do you have the drive to work on that report and do it to the best of your ability? What might get in the way? And crucially if you don't know the answers to those questions (or don't like the answers), who can help you? Who do you know that

'There is never enough time, unless you're serving it.'
Malcolm Forbes

might provide a solution in keeping with your vision of success?

Taking the earlier point of the 'two-way process', there is now the thought of this same formula being applied to a team. How are you going to get everyone in your group or team to work to the same objective? Do you reward or praise or thank your co-workers enough? What problems might they have to prevent them giving their best work and getting the most from you and those around you? These things are usually covered in so many other ways and you are probably doing some of this now in one guise or other, but please ask yourself this – do you reward any one for their 'attitude'?

If you accept the premise that success and achievement are reached with a healthy dose of the right attitude, then surely it is something to encourage? It might surprise someone to thank them for bringing a smile to work but imagine how much you would appreciate being praised for that. I heard a football manager speaking of a new player in his team, he said, *'The lad's a radiater, he always brightens training sessions with his smile. Some players are drainers and some are radiaters – he's a radiater.'*

I imagine an extra spring in the step of that player and perhaps one or two of the others asking themselves some tough questions. (Granted we are talking about footballers so they probably find most questions tough).

But let's get back to you. There will be days when you don't skip to the office and you wonder what you are doing or find yourself racked with self-doubt. These are the times where you have to go back to the first part of the formula – *ability*. Be realistic here, we all lose some

> *'My mother drew a distinction between achievement and success. She said that 'achievement is the knowledge that you have studied and worked hard and done the best that is in you. Success is being praised by others, and that's nice, too, but not as important or satisfying. Always aim for achievement and forget about success.'*
> Helen Hayes

energy now and then but could you really have got where you are without ability? Would you have even chosen your career without some native talent or inherent ability? Don't let these negative thoughts sap your energy, address them and then dismiss them with a cuff round the ears, and move on. Where the doubt is with a co-worker, you might not want to use the last bit – industrial tribunals can have a detrimental effect on a team.

Teaching Trust

It might seem too obvious to mention but being straight with people and earning their trust is one of the most important things to achieve. This is as much to do with never promising more than you can deliver as it is to do with basic honesty. Perhaps the people you work with know you to be trustworthy and your reputation is sound. But it can quickly be eroded if you let someone down and the network principle goes into reverse to send out all the wrong messages. It's looking people in the eye and being what you appear to be.

A lot of people will let you down, that's life. But at least you can learn from the disappointment and ensure you don't make the same mistake. Doing what you do well, being honest and trustworthy, not betraying confidences, and delivering your promises on time, within budget and to a high standard. And if that sounds hard, it should. If it were easy to do, how could you differentiate yourself from the pack? You want it to be hard and for the competition to struggle while you build a reputation for achieving these standards.

There is always a danger that with all these promises and good intentions, you can talk yourself into a corner. If you are talking to a

> *'Success in business requires training and discipline and hard work. But if you're not frightened by these things, the opportunities are just as great today as they ever were.'*
> David Rockefeller

34

potential client or employer be careful not to wax lyrical about what you are going to do instead of what you have already achieved. There are a lot of people with a 'vision' that never get off their collective backsides and actually do anything.

So when you are in this situation, think about the benefits for the other person, don't start talking processes and equipment or boast of the shininess of your new machinery. It won't be long before the whole conversation has become all about you, your future, dreams and ambitions. If you are trying to sell, imagine how you are going to improve the lot of your client or potential client. Think of what they do and how you can make them more profitable, efficient or whatever they might need. And if that can only be done by asking a lot of questions about their business to ascertain their needs, so much the better. Now the conversation is about them and not you.

So what if something does go wrong and the order is going to be delayed through no fault of yours? You really want to ask yourself if it could have been avoided and if it should have been avoided.

Have you ever noticed that successful people never seem to make excuses? Punctual people don't complain about traffic jams, they just allow time for them. If you have some paperwork to do before you leave for a meeting, why not bring it with you and finish it in the car park of your client. That way you have a built-in safety valve for traffic, car problems, or any other variable. Added to which, you walk in to the office of your client relaxed and unruffled.

All of which is good practice, but it is also a metaphor for general business process; be aware of potential problems, look at ways you can stay ahead of them or neutralise the problem and when it comes time to deliver, you do so calmly without appearing that it was all a last

> 'Plans are only good intentions unless they immediately degenerate into hard work.'
>
> Peter Drucker

minute rush and you made the deadline by the skin of your teeth. It is always better to under-promise and over-deliver.

You need to earn respect to earn trust. You must also believe in yourself and your ability, and earn your own self-respect first. With it comes a quiet air of authority which will make all of this come naturally. When you know that you are selling something you believe in, and truly expect your service or process to make a difference to someone else, you really don't need to sell it, just explain it. When you believe in yourself, when you have shaped and modelled yourself into the type of business person, networker or employee you can believe in, you don't need to sell yourself either. Now you are ready to chat and, of course in networking, to listen.

Networking misconceptions

A lot of people who haven't taken the time to think about networking or the trouble to research the possibilities, make the mistake of thinking they already know it all. You get the person who thinks *you only need to hand out your business card*. How often have you come across a business card in your wallet or purse and have absolutely no idea how it got there or to whom it belongs? I know I have. Business cards are important and we will talk about that too, but they are only one tool, not an ultimate solution.

Then there are those that say *they have tried it before and it doesn't work*. Tried it when? This is something you learn how to do, improve your technique, refine your method and then do it all the time wherever you are without thinking about it. Networking is a way to live and improve your life, not something you do for an hour and then dash home in time for 'Holby City'.

> *'Nothing succeeds like the appearance of success.'*
> Christopher Lasch

'I just do my job – I don't need to network at work.' God bless him, this is the person who might have got your next job, and the same person who will be surprised and disappointed when he is passed over for promotion. Every company has these people, just make sure you are not one of them.

There are those who complain that *networking is an 'old boys' club'*. They are right. That's exactly what it is. Except it is not limited to 'old boys' or 'boys' and you don't need a membership card. There has always been a form of networking and when you hear people complaining that the jobs go to people who know people – well – duh! Go out there and meet some people yourself and stop complaining about it. It's easy to assume you are being excluded if you never try to get 'in'. Only if you try and find the way barred can you truly claim to be on the outside of a system.

I have heard people saying, *'you need to be good at networking'*. Does that mean that you can't be good at it or you are not good at it and don't want to make any effort to improve? Like so many things, you get better with practice. Go to some events, talk to your neighbours, then come back and think about how it was handled in relation to the things you have learned and consider how it could have been better handled. You will soon be as good as you want to be.

Some believe that *it's all shiny suits* over white sport socks and black shoes with those wee buckles. If you ever enter a meeting and are met with a room full of shiny suited, brylcreemed, white-socked, buckly people, you have my full permission to turn and run. (Unless you work for the company that makes the shoe buckles in which case you are about to get what you deserve.) There is just no 'type' as far as networking is concerned; it depends on the target market, the venue, the city and the amount of free hospitality. Just make sure you pick the right one.

> *'People forget how fast you did a job –*
> *but they remember how well you did it.'*
> Howard Newton

The *free hospitality* is another myth of networking; especially in these days of sensible drink-driving practice, you will find a lot of events with tables of tea, coffee and fruit juice. Also little biscuits from Marks and Spencer's. Another good tip is to go for the wee, lozenge-shaped, brown, wrinkly, chocolate biscuits, they don't look much but they are soooo tasty!

Does networking cost a lot of money? Surprisingly, no. If we think specifically of networking events – people want you there, companies want you there and usually someone is sponsoring the event whether it's the government or someone trying to sell you something. What they cost you is time, and that's the price you have to pay. You can always tape 'Holby City'.

So is it hard work? Not if you are doing it right. If you follow the precepts laid out in this book and take them to heart, you can relax and enjoy every second. Things tend to be hard work when you are struggling, when they come naturally and they are what you want to do – especially when you do them well – they are more often thoroughly enjoyable. Just make sure you leave yourself time to have a life or how else can you chat about your unicycle riding?

I have even heard of those people who are discouraged because they thought they had to be funny or entertaining. Hopefully that is a myth I dispelled early on here. Networking is always more about listening than talking, or if you want to be cynical, laughing rather than telling a joke. Be a good audience, not the main attraction.

There are so many myths and misconceptions, too many to go into, people who think it's not for them or not relevant or that it's all lawyers and accountants that do it (if you are a lawyer or an accountant, there

> *'Real success is finding your lifework in the work that you love.'*
> David McCullough

probably are lots of events for you too) but don't worry if some people don't understand or approve, it just means more opportunity for you.

Maintain strategic networks of centres of influence

If we have got a bit soft and fluffy for a bit, let's toughen up.

Without stepping back from our commitment to help other companies as a strategy for building our own name and reputation, let's not forget we want to be the best we can be and to make some money. Don't be afraid to admit this, it doesn't make you a bad person, just an honest one.

So I want you to be a shark. Eyes front, looking forward and meeting opposition head on. Remember that a shark must always move forward or it will drown. Leave your previous mistakes behind you, don't hang on to past achievements, look to new challenges and new goals.

You are reading a book that you want to help you with new goals and you want to use networking as a tool for success. Don't stop planning now. Think about what else you need. Who will be in your sphere of influence and are there areas where you need help? Maintain those spheres, plan to keep in contact with the people you need in place. Put notes in your diary to get in touch with someone if you haven't heard from them in a while. Keep the spheres moving forward now that you have started.

Only approximately 1 in 50 connections will generate monetary rewards. The remaining 49 connections generate knowledge, kindness, politeness, peace of mind and if you are lucky some nice lunches but most importantly generate your reputation

> *'Pleasure in the job puts perfection in the work.'*
> Aristotle

John D Rockefeller, the great oil magnate who created Esso, always reminded everyone about their reputation. He said, *'when you take away all my money and all my assets, the only thing I have is my reputation.'*

Long-term networking

Of course, it would be lovely if you put down this book, walked in to a networking event and were fabulously wealthy and popular by the end of the week. But just in case it doesn't happen, let's think about a slightly longer strategy.

Think of all the successful people who have tried and failed and kept going until somebody gave them their big chance. Before going on to sell tens of millions of books around the world, *'To Kill A Mockingbird'* was rejected by several publishers. Fred Astaire was described on his first audition as someone who 'can't act, can't sing, can dance a bit', the Wright Brothers were told they would never get their project off the ground – the list is endless. I can imagine the guy who invented the wheel facing a load of primitive types grunting, 'I liked the old square shape. Uggh.' So don't allow anyone else to put you down or take the wind from your sails, just pity their poor judgement and move on to the next opportunity.

Remember too that we live in a world of communication, so look for ways to reach the global community and think of your network not in terms of those you can drive to meet but everyone who has access to a computer or mobile phone. Be a village in a global economy – build local and sell global and have a vision of where you are going – even in times of darkness. Keep being positive.

Be positive even when you don't feel it inside. There will be times

> *'If for some reason you are not happy for yourself, try and be happy for those people who are happy. Happiness is infectious - you will get better.'*
> James Alexander

when you doubt yourself but that's okay, we all do that sometimes. Get over it, move on, move ahead.

You need to be a big-picture person when networking. Remember you don't know what lead or connection or phone call or business card will give you a chance or opportunity, so spread them far and wide like those little cards tied to balloons or messages in bottles and let them drift ever outwards. And is it not exciting, the thought that out there somewhere, there might just be a collision of chance which will find its way home to you? Perhaps the longer it takes, just reflects the length of the journey.

Don't believe that people are natural born winners. Some people, winners, just make it look that way because they are confident and positive. We all make mistakes sometimes, have our set backs and disappointments, it's what happens next that determines your future.

Keep learning, keep improving, keep moving forward, stay positive and the longer it takes the more you will feel that sense of pride that comes with hard work and focus.

'The policy of being too cautious is the greatest risk of all.'
Jawaharlal Nehru

3

Networking is Gossiping with a Purpose

Let's be honest- we all enjoy a bit of a gossip, but just think, now you can do it with a purpose and a good purpose at that. When we are talking about people and what they are doing and have done, but doing it in a positive way, everyone benefits. We are not only maintaining our spheres of influence but expanding them and helping others with theirs. The more informed our contacts, the more they can add to the pool of knowledge and the more effective they are in their own networks.

If their networks are extensions of our own then a good blether can be a force of good for growth. There is no downside to this ripple effect and everyone in the pool continues to gain from reinforcing their information. Another important thing to remember is that you can only benefit from the way everyone within these networks bonds. Don't think, 'Hey! Wait a minute – that's my friend!' because the stronger the strands of the network, the better for all.

It all comes back to **who** you know, not what you know. The more we do it, the more we learn. For instance, you can tell someone of an

---

'Respect yourself and others will respect you.'
Confucius

43

accountant who has just started a new business. You tell someone about her, perhaps point out that she is still establishing her business and is keen to bring in new clients. The person you are talking to might tell you of a friend with a small printing firm who could do some business cards or a web designer that could help her. The printer gets in touch and tells the accountant of some business cards he is doing for another new start-up who could use an accountant or the accountant tells of a client looking for some flyers. And as it grows and you keep in touch with everyone, see how they are doing and offer your services.

You have just helped two or three companies and expanded your network, and you mention to the next person you talk to that you know of a web designer who is doing some fast effective work with an accountant you know and a printer who has just started doing some menus for a new restaurant. If you can't get a free meal by the time the week's out you just aren't trying hard enough.

There is another side to this process and an important one. If you do end up sipping chardonnay in a new bistro and the food is cold, the service surly and the menu (however well printed) uninspiring, you have to be honest. Remember you want to establish your own integrity and blindly recommending the services of everyone you bump into in the street will lead to other people questioning your judgement. That will inevitably lead to your own reputation being tarnished. Sometimes that's not easy; you might like the restaurateur personally and want him to succeed but if you send all your contacts to his restaurant and they have a bad experience you will lose credibility.

> 'Regard your good name as the richest jewel you can possibly be possessed of - for credit is like fire; when once you have kindled it you may easily preserve it, but if you once extinguish it, you will find it an arduous task to rekindle it again. The way to gain a good reputation is to endeavour to be what you desire to appear.'
>
> Socrates

Making contact with the right person can also be a challenge as it's not always the most obvious person in a company with whom you want to establish a rapport. You may be on lunching terms with the procurement manager of a large company but if his PA can't stand you, it could be difficult to find time in his diary for a meeting.

Sometimes, sadly, you must also be aware of office politics and if by befriending one person you are alienated from another, it's important to know it. I am not suggesting you chose between the two on the basis of which is the most useful but, by not knowing of a rift, you may inadvertently find yourself in a situation where neither person will trust you and assume you favour the other 'camp'. Subtle diplomacy is probably the best tactic to employ here (or to put it another way, sit on the fence!).

Shiny plastic business cards and who were you exactly?

If there is one tool most associated with networking, it has to be the business card. For that reason alone it should not be overlooked or minimised. Perhaps the people you meet will judge you on your own card? So what does it say about you? Is it clearly laid out with your name displayed prominently and clearly? Perhaps it has your picture on it, and your email address? Does it have the name of your company and address and the head office and VAT number and the contact details for your dentist in case of emergency? All that on a small rectangular card! Amazing. I guess our cards really do say more about us than we always intend, so it's all the more important that you think what message you are sending out.

> 'One can survive everything, nowadays, except death, and live down everything except a good reputation.'
>
> Oscar Wilde

Also will you please double check and triple check the contact details are correct. I came across a mortgage adviser who had the wrong email address on his business card. It's like a metaphor for all our networking – making the right impression, conveying what we do and who we are but trying not to bore the pants off everyone we meet.

So make sure you get across the basic facts and make it easy for anyone who looks at your card to remember who you are and what you do for a living. But don't then leave your cards in a box in your office; make sure you keep them with you all the time. I try to keep cards in all my handbags and car and briefcase, you never know when you might run in to someone and want to exchange business cards.

> I was a keynote speaker at a business conference in a hotel in the North of Scotland a couple of years ago and went for a swim in the hotel pool. I struck up a conversation with a fellow swimmer and ended up talking about business and networking (and no, you don't need to tell me how sad it is that I can't even go for a swim without making new contacts) but neither of us had thought to pack our business cards in our swimming costumes. I do confess that my mind immediately turned to getting some specially laminated cards for such an occasion before realising that it was time I got a life!

So, that's your own card sorted, but what do you do with the cards you receive? They must also be considered an important part of the process of meeting and maintaining your network. I like to make a note on the back of each card so that I remember where and when I met the person and perhaps a note to remind me a little about them. I try to avoid 'short dark haired man' as that never seems to narrow the field much (I am 6ft 1") and I am paranoid that the card is ever

> 'A good reputation is more valuable than money.'
> Publilius Syrus, *Maxims*

seen by the person who donated it – can you imagine the danger? 'Wee dark-haired bloke with bad breath and personal hygiene problems' – it might just signal the end of a beautiful friendship.

I also like to organise my cards so that I can locate them later.

My own system is to keep them alphabetically (I use first names because it's what I remember more easily) but separate the cards I refer to most often; these I keep on a notice board near my desk. The board also has the cards of people I intend phoning in the next few days as a type of prompter.

The Japanese have a very formal approach to exchanging business cards which we could all learn from; when you are handed a card, actually look at it. This might seem obvious but it's very easy to glance at it, say thanks and stuff in a pocket or wallet. Make it clear to the person giving you the card that you value it (and by extension, them) and read it, thank them by name, look them in the face, and then put it away carefully. (You can always toss it in the bin later – NOT !!) Note also that Chinese people offer and accept cards with both hands, holding the card in front of them, between forefingers and thumbs. Do the same and you will be seen as a worthy colleague.

Six degrees of separation

This is something I find really fascinating and often use in my networking workshops as a demonstration. Who would you like to meet with for five minutes? When I ask this question I get answers like Margaret Thatcher, Robbie Williams, George Clooney (girls, you know what I mean. George if you read this, my agent is waiting for your call), Richard Branson, Stelios, Bill Gates and so on. So then you ask if anyone knows anyone who knows someone who … The

> *'You can't build a reputation on what you are going to do.'*
> Henry Ford

amazing thing is how simply and in how few steps it is possible to find a way to get in touch with just about anyone.

This theory is called the Six Degrees of Separation. The original 'six degrees of separation' was first proposed in 1967 by sociologist Stanley Milgram who called it the 'small world phenomenon'. Milgram asked 96 randomly selected people around the country to send a piece of mail to an acquaintance, who would send the mail along to another acquaintance, in an attempt to reach a designated 'target' person in Boston. The messages that actually made it to their destination passed through an average of six people.

Since then we have had the more common usage of the internet both at home and at work and I wondered if I could actually beat those 6 moves. I decided to have a little experiment myself. But first it needed some careful consideration. I live in the UK and have also lived in Hong Kong – so to be fair, I wanted to try this experiment with someone who lived outside of the UK and Europe, preferably not in Asia and probably not someone who lived in the USA as I could have used my friends from school to help me there.

I decided that the person that I would try and contact within the 6 moves was Nelson Mandela as he lived on a continent and in a country where I had no direct connections and I have never visited. I was so delighted that I had fixed 'my target contact person' that I told a friend of mine who was on MSN Messenger at the time. Dom told me to stop in my tracks as I had already completed the move in 2! He had a friend in South Africa who knew Nelson Mandela personally – so within 30 seconds of deciding, I actually had a telephone number for Mr Mandela which I dialled...

If you make a plan and know who you want to reach, it will surprise

---

'A good name, like good will, is got by many actions and lost by one.'
Lord Jeffery

you how 'reachable' that person might be. I like to think of this as 'People Mapping' and it is worth giving a little thought.

Sometimes taking a step back from what you are doing, deciding what and who you need and what advice you could use and where to get it is a useful exercise. Draw out a little map and put you at one end and the person who you think could most give you the advice or information which might make a difference to your business. Now think who might know someone that might have a way of getting in touch with that person. Have a look through your contacts, speak to members of your personal network, and start to add people to your map. You will be amazed at how few steps it will take to put you in touch with your target. Of course you may also receive a restraining order for stalking so tread softly.

Entering a crowded room and not knowing anyone

Another common fear for anyone embarking on their first networking foray is entering a room full of strangers. How do you get to talk to anyone, or break in to a group of people without appearing rude? Will you be left alone standing in the corner with no one talking to you?

Think this way – there are three types of people:

☺ Those who make things happen.

😐 Those who watch things happen, and

☹ Those who wondered what happened.

Sometimes you just have to walk up to a group and say, 'Help! I don't know anyone here.'

'It is better to know some of the questions than all of the answers.'
James Thurber

Remember to make yourself look approachable too. There is no point bemoaning the fact no one is talking to you if your face is scowling and everyone in the room is just plain scared of you or you are standing texting or talking on your mobile phone. Smile, turn your phone off and go over and get a tea or a coffee. The refreshment table is a good place to pick off people and get chatting if for no other reason than they are away from their comfort zone.

Inevitably, in a room full of people chatting, they stand in circular groups which discourage anyone joining them. But remember that is only the natural way for a group to converse and if another person joins them they will widen the circle, not close ranks and keep you out. Don't forget to see if there is a specific person you want to meet and where they are in the room. When you are at a meeting designed for networking, and most business meetings are, either openly or subtly, everyone there wants to talk to you. If you don't know anyone there, and they are not talking to you, how can you take it personally?

If you go in to a room full of colleagues and no one talks to you, just leave – they clearly don't like you. But if all you need is an introduction in a room full of strangers, look for someone else who might be in need of rescue, and introduce yourself. Once you are talking, you will usually find someone else will join you, and before long the problem is solved. (Now you can pass the time sniggering at anyone else arriving with no one talking to them.)

A simple and very effective way to solve this problem is to arrive early at an event, or even (shock, horror) be the first person to arrive. Not only will you get to chat to the organisers, who will be glad to see you and get the event up and running, but when others arrive, it will be easy and natural to chat to them and they will assume that you know other people or even the hosts, as they saw you chatting when they

> 'Getting ahead in a difficult profession requires avid faith in yourself. That is why some people with mediocre talent, but with great inner drive, go much further than people with vastly superior talent.'
> Sophia Loren

shuffled in to the room. Let's hope that not too many people buy this book or I can see this getting out of hand as everyone feels they must go earlier and earlier to an event just to be the first there.

Be in the room

How many times have you arrived at an event or conference or even a meeting and put your mobile phone setting to 'silent' or 'vibrate'. You don't want to miss a call or find that someone tried to get you and you were otherwise engaged. That also means that there is part of your attention, no matter where you are or what you are doing, taken up with that potential call. That also means by extension that you are not giving your full attention to what you are doing, or really listening to the person in front of you. BE IN THE ROOM, don't be partly there and partly with that possible client or colleague. Turning off your mobile phone is not the same as turning off 'life support' there will not be any dire consequences. If the call you think might be coming is more important than the person you are talking to, the meeting you are attending or the lecture you are listening to, then don't go to the meeting, don't be in the room.

This can be extended to everything you do in business and networking. Is there anything more irritating than being in the middle of an enthralling conversation only to have the other person's mobile start to ring, whereupon he or she make some excuse and go off to start a conversation with someone else. I will grant you there are exceptions to this rule where someone explains they are waiting for an important call, apologises for their rudeness and make a point of getting back as soon as possible and resuming the chat. Too often though you feel that you are less important than anyone who chooses to dial the other person's number. Remember that feeling the next

> 'Whatever you are by nature, keep to it; never desert your line of talent. Be what nature intended you for and you will succeed.'
> Sydney Smith

time you think of leaving your phone turned on no matter what setting you use.

Extend this attitude to everything you do and you will see a marked improvement in your efficiency. If you have children who are looking for your attention, don't palm them off because you have work to do, or be in the same room with them but not actually 'in the room'. Don't be there in body only, be there in mind, body and spirit, and if you are distracted, ask yourself why. This also forces you to deal with the things you need to do or make provision for getting them done.

You can too easily fool yourself that you are dealing with something simply because you haven't yet dismissed it. You either have time to get everything done or you should find a way to do that whether that means delegating or changing your priorities. What does all this have to do with networking? When you have the opportunity to be with a member of your network or someone who might extend your network, don't waste the chance because you are not focused on what they are saying or blow it completely by excusing yourself to talk to someone on your mobile. When you are networking, where ever you are doing it, *be in the room.*

Improving your attitude through body language

According to research, 65% of communication is non verbal.

Or to put it another way, body language is more important than you might believe. As ever, this is a two-way street, and learning what other people are saying is vital, but no more than being sure you are saying what you intend to say.

'Put yourself on view. This brings your talents to light.'
Baltasar Gracian

With practice and experience, you can become a polyglot of body language but let me demonstrate with some straightforward examples:

- The way you make eye contact with someone shows levels of trust and honesty.
  It shows that you value their opinion and are interested in what they have to say and respect them. It also shows confidence (or a lack thereof) and if someone can't meet your eye and proffers a limp, damp hand to shake, part of you no longer wants anything to do with this person. So the secret is to make a lot of eye contact without 'freaking out' the person you are talking to – the image you are seeking is 'attentive' not 'psycho'.

- The way you stand is important too; don't fidget, or keep looking around the room when someone is talking to you. Try not to slouch (and, yes, I know I sound like your third grade teacher). Good posture helps you appear confident and alert. In a long evening of being on your feet, it will also help your breathing and energy levels.

- Head position – now I am not saying that you have got to look as if you are just out of a military academy – but a good head means good business. By keeping a straight position, this gives you authority, and what you are saying can be taken seriously. If you want to appear friendly, you may want to tilt your head a little to one side.

- Distance from others is crucial. You want to give off the right signals and not appear pushy nor invade someone's personal space. Generally, in UK society, the first 18 inches of space

'You must keep sending work out; you must never let a manuscript do nothing but eat its head off in a drawer. You send that work out again and again, while you're working on another one. If you have talent, you will receive some measure of success - but only if you persist.'
Isaac Asimov

surrounding people is reserved for lovers, boxers and muggers, apart from the initial handshake (or if you follow the ever more popular Continental approach, the right-side-left-side mwaah-kiss). This distance keeping is even more important if you had a large portion of garlic bread at lunch. If you move into someone's space, and they step back, then you are probably too close. The other thing that you do not want to do is appear stand-offish either.

- Try not to fidget or look as though you would rather be talking to someone else. Your feet shuffling might hint that they want to be taking you off on their way to another part of the room. The next time you are having a pleasant conversation with someone you know and like, take a mental snapshot of the way they are standing and the way you are standing, the position of your head, what you are doing with your hands and any of a dozen things that we all do without being especially aware of them. By re-creating the way you feel at those times, you are being yourself and giving off good positive vibes and you are doing it in a way that is natural for you. There is no point in copying the way a famous film star poses if you feel a complete fool doing it.

Of course what you really want to learn is if someone is trustworthy and if you can rely on what they are telling you. So here is the pocket Lie Test, just for you.

You have probably heard the expression, *'Speak no evil, see no evil, hear no evil'* which is usually illustrated with three monkeys?

Well, keep this phrase in mind if you are in a business meeting with someone and you are trying to assess the other person. You will usually find that your gut reaction is correct about a person, but here are a few pointers.

> *'Integrity without knowledge is weak and useless, and knowledge without integrity is dangerous and dreadful.'*
>
> **Samuel Johnson**

- When people are lying (or being economical with the truth), they tend to speak one thing while blocking the words with their hands almost as though their hands are on strike, blockading the words coming from the mouth.

- 'See no evil'; repeatedly rubbing their eyes is another sign that they are not comfortable with what they are saying, while 'hear no evil' is represented by a continual rubbing of the ears or playing with the lobes while talking.

- There are people who can glibly say one thing while thinking another, but the body never lies! Watch for these signs for yourself and be careful if you have an itchy eye when you are going in to a meeting – it might be misinterpreted!

Next time you are in a meeting that you are not hosting or speaking at, have a look at the body language of the participants. It will be very interesting to see (and endeavour to interpret) what different types of body language are going on around the table.

Overleaf are some body language hints.

'Real integrity is doing the right thing, knowing that nobody's going to know whether you did it or not.'
Oprah Winfrey, in *Good Housekeeping*

ENGAGING	LISTENING	BORED	WANTS TO SPEAK
Leaning forward	Head tilted	Staring into space	Finger tapping
Open body	Lots of eye contact	Slumped posture	Foot tapping
Open arms	Nodding	Doodling	Staring
Open hands	High blink rate	Foot tapping	
KEEN / EAGER	**EVALUATING**	**LET ME GET OUT OF HERE**	**AGGRESSIVE**
Open legs	Sucks glasses / pencil	Feet towards the door	Leaning forwards
Feet under chair	Strokes chin	Looking around	Finger pointing
On toes	Looks up and right	Buttoning jacket	Fists clenched
Leaning forward	Ankle on knee		
READY TO AGREE	**ATTENTIVE**	**LYING**	
Closes papers	Open feet	Touches face	
Pen down	Smile	Pulls ear	
Hands flat on table	Arms behind back	Hand over mouth	
		Eyes down	
		Looks down and left	

A basic must with regards to body language for networking and any social or business meetings is the easiest one – smile and more often than not others will smile back.

> *'The strongest principle of growth lies in human choice.'*
> George Eliot

Conversational prompts

Now that you are standing comfortably, let's move on to what you are saying; sustaining a conversation is not always straightforward. I would like to suggest a few pointers for doing it well. I mentioned before in my 'myths of networking' that you are not expected to be funny and entertaining, but you don't want to feel you are being a bore.

By listening properly you can be a sponge – absorbing a tremendous amount of information. We begin our careers with an empty notebook and that is the exact same thing as networking – you begin with a blank page.

When presented with a new contact, you will want to ask business questions, personal questions or at times what they think of the rainfall for the time of year. It is often more important how you phrase the question than the specifics of what you are asking.

Remember you are not cross-examining the other person, but trying to engage them in conversation, and the more relaxed and comfortable that conversation, the more positive the outcome. So don't ask closed questions but give your subject the opportunity to talk to you. Let me illustrate:

You: 'Isn't this weather terrible?'

Subject: 'Yes'

You: 'Don't you just hate the constant rain?'

Subject: 'Yes'.

You: 'It's not been much of a summer, eh?'

'Curiosity killed the cat, but for a while I was a suspect.'
Steven Wright

Subject: 'No'

You: 'If I keep this line of conversation up, you will soon want to kill yourself, right?'

Subject: 'Yes'

Wow, you were really terrible there, so try again.

You: 'Do you know if the rain is forecast to go on all week?'

Subject: 'No idea, I never watch the weather.'

You: 'Do you avoid all tv or is it something personal about the met office?'

Subject: 'I just don't watch television'

You: 'So what do you do to unwind of an evening?'

Subject: 'I am the grand warlock of a devil worshipping sect.'

You: 'Fascinating, but I think I just saw someone that owes me money, excuse me....'

There you go now, had you not asked some pertinent questions in the right way you might have wasted precious time talking to him.

Journalists are taught at an early stage to ask enough questions and in the correct way to ensure they don't miss an important aspect of the story.

In any situation where you are asking questions on any subject, find out the following:

? Who (get them to name names)

> 'The cure for boredom is curiosity. There is no cure for curiosity.'
> Dorothy Parker

? Where (places, buildings, countries)

? When (times and dates can be important)

? What (make sure you are specific)

? How (remember you want them to talk, asking them how they did it might be the question that gives most scope to blether).

Of course, you are not trying to 'catch them out' in order to sell their story in the tabloid newspapers but if you ask questions at all, make sure you are listening to the reply. There is no more irritating person than the one who asks you a question and on your reply asks another question to which, had they been listening, they would already known the answer.

You (again):   'Do you come here often'

Subject: 'No they hadn't built it when I was incarcerated fifteen years ago, and I only got out last week when the pardon came through from the home secretary and the press finally stopped hounding me for a statement this morning so I thought I would go out for a quiet drink to celebrate my release.'

You: 'Have you been away on holiday yet this year, you look a bit pale?'

Try instead to *really listen* to what they are saying and follow up with a question to encourage them to expand on what they have told you. If someone tells you their wife has just had a baby, don't say, 'Really? So what did you think of the football at the weekend?'

That's an extreme example but we can all make the mistake of not

'I've learned that you can't have everything and do everything at the same time.'
Oprah Winfrey, in *O Magazine*

realising that someone is keen to tell you about a subject that matters to them. Often a simple, modest reply can be a plea to ask them to tell more:

You: 'What did you get up to at the weekend?'

Subject: 'I was at my daughter's school prize giving.'

You: 'Really? How is she doing?'

Subject: 'We are so proud of her; she has been made captain of her house hockey team and is torn between offers from Oxford and Cambridge Universities for next term, though personally we feel she would benefit from finishing her first year at senior school...'

And when you get a detailed response to a question, there is usually enough material (if you were listening) to ensure that sustaining a lively conversation will be no problem. The important ingredient is 'listening', not the quality of the questions. Listen to what they say, what they seem to avoid saying, their body language (sometimes if someone crosses their arms and steps back it would suggest you have strayed on to a subject that makes them uncomfortable) and make sure the next thing you ask reflects that you were listening and not simply preparing a follow-up question.

Active listening is a real skill and as such will improve with practice. The good news is that you can practise anywhere any time. If you are stuck in a post office queue and strike up a conversation with the pensioner behind you, see if you can control the conversation, put him at his ease, and when you are (finally) served, you go away knowing a little about him and who he is, what he did for a living perhaps, or at the very least his name. It might not get you the business lead that will

'Isn't everyone a part of everyone else?'
Budd Schulberg, in *O Magazine*

turn your company around or get you that promotion, but the chances are you will have made someone's day a little more interesting and made a new friend.

'Try to learn something about everything and everything about something.'

Thomas Hardy

4

How to Network Effectively

We have discussed body language, but there is also your tone of voice and what impression your words give. The words themselves will provide the information but the way you say them will colour the image you project. You want to make it clear that you are the type of person who gets things done; make it clear that you have a 'can-do' attitude and a quiet determination to meet deadlines and fulfil briefs. Try to be friendly but not superficial and strong willed without appearing an arrogant bully. You want to appear the sort of person that others can work with and whose company and advice they might seek.

Within an organisation, a successful manager will draw on the experience and networking abilities of those around him, so it helps to be aware of how other people network. Not only can you learn from the way someone else approaches the challenges (or learn how not to do it where it is done badly) but you can tap in to their network and experience to strengthen your own.

Pay it forward – the principle

The Pay it Forward principle was started in June 2000 by Catherine Ryan Hyde in the States, and she has since established a charitable

'Never trust the advice of a man in difficulties.'

Aesop

foundation that promotes the basic principles espoused in her novel.

But her own Pay It Forward experience occurred almost 24 years ago. Ryan Hyde was living in Los Angeles in a 'tough' neighbourhood, and late one night her car stalled on a ramp leading off a freeway. Before she knew it, her car was filled with smoke and the engine was on fire. She then observed two men running toward her with a blanket. They quickly popped the car's bonnet and did what they could to extinguish the flames. At the same time, a fire engine appeared on the scene. It all happened so fast that Ryan Hyde was unable to thank the two men, who disappeared into the night.

To this day, she doesn't know who they were. But at that same moment the Pay It Forward concept started to develop in her mind as Ryan Hyde realised she owed a huge debt of gratitude to someone. *'It seemed like too much to do for a total stranger,'* she told Rotarians. *'I was later told that we could have been killed. These two gentlemen probably saved my life, and they risked their own lives. And I don't even know who they are.'*

In practice, 'paying it forward' often means that when you get 'paid back' for a favour you did for someone or a kind deed, it comes to you tenfold – people are always more grateful for a selfless deed than they are for a 'favour' that has a specific response or payment in mind. And it's a lovely way to live your life, making other people happy and knowing that when the time comes, they will look forward to making you happy too. Not because they owe you, just because they recognise it's what you would do if the roles were reversed.

It's all about using your experience, networking skills, contacts and everything that entails and recognising where it can be of help to others.

'In the business world, the rearview mirror is always clearer than the windshield.'

Warren Buffett

A friendly warning: the opposite is just as true, if you let people down, use them and lie to them, they will always remember you for it and if and when the time comes as eventually it always does, they will pay you back. Tenfold.

Putting a different spin on what you do

Are you an accountant or are you someone who saves their clients £1,000 a year?

Do you cut hair or are you an artist who makes people feel good about themselves? Put a different spin on describing yourself and show what is good about what you do and by extension why you care, and the thing that makes you good at your chosen profession. Someone who just 'cuts hair' is marking time until they clock off, but the artist is someone with enthusiasm and energy and there is really no choice between the two if you are in the market for a short back and sides.

Tongue-tied and twisted

When life hands you a lemon? Have a tequila ...

Ten ways to stand out in a crowd

1. Alex Ferguson, manager of Manchester United Football Club (probably former manager by the time you read this book) has this advice to give on running a new business: *'Work hard and be punctual'*
   Project that image and you are already up and running. And look at it this way – if you want to be noticed in a company, it's better

> *'I ran the wrong kind of business, but I did it with integrity.'*
> Sydney Biddle Barrows, in Marian Christy, *'Mayflower Madam Tells All,'* Boston Globe

to be seen in the office when no one else has arrived yet, than when you come charging through the door in the middle of a meeting because you slept in.

2. Let your personality shine through, and if that means a bit of cheek, or a dash of charm, or flash of confidence, so be it. Don't hide yourself away and then be surprised when you are overlooked.

3. Be enthusiastic (it's a hugely infectious quality), be nosey and be sure that everyone knows who you are. Not everyone will like you for it or admire your confidence, wit, cheek or even enthusiasm. But remember that the only thing worse than people talking badly of you is people not talking about you at all.

4. A smiling person is judged to be more pleasant, attractive, sincere, sociable and competent than a non-smiling grouch.

5. People will buy into your idea if they understand – keep it simple. Practice your FAB pitch (see page 76) and get it down to two or three short, simple, concise sentences.

6. Believe in yourself – your own brand. Understand your role, deliver your brand, translate that brand – what you stand for and what are your promises.

7. Do not brag about how good you are, or your dreams or your riches.

9. Networking more often than not involves eating or drinking – you want to be memorable – and there are some memories which are better than others.

10. Be polite. Manners cost nothing so treat everyone as you would

---

'My own business always bores me to death; I prefer other people's.'
Oscar Wilde in *Lady Windermere's Fan*

wish to be treated yourself. People like to buy from – and recommend – people that they like.

Who were you again?

While you are going all-out to be remembered and memorable, be sure not to forget the people you meet yourself. Don't be one of those who dismiss their inability to remember someone's name with the phrase, 'oh I'm terrible with names but I never forget a face.'

Learn to remember names. It's not good enough to forget names and expect others to think that you remember them (their face or anything else) because how can you then pretend they are important to you if you didn't even take enough notice of them to know their name? The flipside of this is that people are often pleasantly surprised that you do remember them and ideally some details of what they do or the names of their children.

If you really cannot remember someone's name (no brownie points for you!), you could use our publisher's ploy. He would ask the person for his name and, when told, would say, 'Of course, I remember your first name – it was the surname that escaped me.' Or the other way round, if that seems more appropriate. Don't do it too often, though!

Now you can genuinely go on to talk to them and convince them you are pleased to see them and have a relationship beyond the simple pleasantries. Don't too readily assume that they actually remember you, though. If you stride towards someone and start revisiting a conversation you had in a lift six years ago and go on to ask how their five children, dog, cat and pet hamster are doing, and at some point see them fidgeting uncomfortably while edging towards the door, there is every chance they don't know who you are!

> *'I find it rather easy to portray a businessman. Being bland, rather cruel and incompetent comes naturally to me.'*
> John Cleese

If you do walk up to someone and say, 'Hi James, Lindsay Bannerman – we met in the lift in April 1993, how is your cold coming along...?' I guarantee they will automatically respond 'Lindsay! Of course I remember you ...' but you will see the look of relief on their face nonetheless.

The art of being interested

Too many people work hard at being interesting – what you need to do is refine the art of being *interested*. It sounds easy – just tilt your head to one side in a reflective, yet studied way, and look intently in to the eyes of the person talking to you while remembering to maintain good posture and not yawn. Now what did they just say? Try to put other thoughts out of your head and not to be thinking of your next question or who you are going to approach next or wonder if the person you are talking to is aware of the spinach on her teeth.

These are things we all do, so don't feel too bad, just try instead to really listen to what the other person is saying. Try to mesh with their enthusiasm, keep your mind open and let them convince you. After all, they are doing all the work, you only need to listen and if you are attentive it should be no problem asking a pertinent question when they stop for breath.

Listening in networking

Everything we are doing here is related to listening. It's not just appearing interested but wondering how to use the information you are receiving. If someone is excitedly relating an idea or a product or a service, you want to be thinking 'who else do I know that could benefit/help with this idea?'

> 'To succeed as a team is to hold all of the members accountable for their expertise.'
> Mitchell Caplan, CEO, E*Trade Group Inc.

What if you know of a venture capitalist or business angel that could help someone to get a new product or invention off the drawing board and in to the market place? What if you know of an invention that someone is trying to get in to the market place and you find yourself talking to someone who wants to invest some venture capital? Or a graphic designer who could provide the packaging for a product? Someone with a haulage company who could distribute the product.

The more your network grows, the more you will find yourself the spider in the middle of a huge web of opportunity. You can only do this if you are listening- really thinking about what you are being told and what you can add by bringing your experience and contacts to the problem.

'The only thing to do with good advice is pass it on. It is never any use to oneself.'

Oscar Wilde

5

Rich and Famous
or Poor and Obscure?

I mentioned earlier the beauty of being nosy, but let's make that 'curious'; having an interest in what is happening around you and being able to tap in to the subsequent flow of information is another thing that makes a great networker. Take a real interest in what you hear in the office, what others volunteer to you, no matter how casual the conversation.

If you remain curious, then you will also want to know what happens next. If someone told you they were considering a new career path last month, what happened? Did they chicken out? Perhaps there is now a position that needs to be filled and you know someone who could do the job. Perhaps a 'career change' means a new business or someone looking for some training and you know some trainers. New premises and you know a property developer.

Every time something changes within your growing network, new opportunities present themselves. New information means a good reason to talk to other people in your network. Remember there is such a thing as positive gossiping when it is done to spread positive information.

> *'There's no business like show business, but there are several businesses like accounting.'*
> David Letterman

71

There is a danger of making everything you are doing sound calculating and networkers incredibly self-obsessed and always looking out for themselves, but that is not my vision of good networking. So many of the good things that come to you through networking are unexpected and from directions that you just didn't see coming. When you build a relationship, you don't need to know it is something or someone that can do something for you. On the contrary, it is often the case that you build relationships for the future. It's like seeing a road you have never travelled and being curious, you drive down it and find out where it goes. It goes nowhere that is of any use to you. A year later you make a new contact in a new part of town and you discover that the quickest way to get there is along that road.

In relationships you don't only make friends with people or businesses that are immediately useful to you – you form these friendships with people because you are interested in where they are going and wish them well. Sometime in the future the path they have taken might just turn out to be somewhere you want to go. Or am I over-extending this metaphor? Be grateful I didn't bring in traffic cones and contra-flows!

Raising your profile – advertising you

Many's the time I don my fishnets and rubber micro skirt with matching ankle boots and go out on the street to sell myself. Hmmm.

Selling yourself is about raising your profile so that people know who you are or have heard your name. It's amazing just how much difference it makes when you are introducing yourself if the other person has heard of you or at least heard your name. For a start, they are more likely to remember you in the future and especially if you make a good impression.

> *'The best and safest thing is to keep a balance in your life, acknowledge the great powers around us and in us. If you can do that, and live that way, you are really a wise man.'*
>
> Euripides

There are many ways of doing this from the blatant type of advertising like putting your face on posters (some estate agents actually put their faces on the boards of houses for sale – terrific idea if you are planning to stand in the next election) to more subtle approaches such as writing to newspapers to express opinions on subjects related to your profession or interests, appearing on radio stations (I am a regular contributor to discussion programmes on BBC Radio Scotland) and posting thoughts and opinions on internet notice boards. Another way of raising your profile is by writing articles for magazines and submitting them with your photograph which means that you can get free advertising too. Many editors are more than happy to receive articles as long as it is not a blatant sales spin. Keep it to a topic that you are an expert in or the field that you work in, in business. Don't keep your thoughts to yourself- get them out there working for you.

Presenting yourself – first impressions count

Have a cold, hard look at yourself in the mirror. What kind of impression do you make? You wouldn't go to work as a bank manager dressed in a mini-skirt and cowboy boots, that's clear (I am proud of resisting the temptation to say – 'especially if you are a bloke'). And yet there are so many less obvious ways that you can give the wrong impression. Are you trying to portray yourself as a young dynamic entrepreneur but wearing a cartoon tie? It was funny for about two days in the eighties. Do you need a haircut? Are you wearing a little too much bling? If you have a cycle company selling yourself on your environment friendly alternative lifestyle, don't turn up at a meeting in a six litre four-by-four.

Really be hard on yourself and seek out the opinion of honest friends;

> 'Success in business requires training and discipline and hard work. But if you're not frightened by these things, the opportunities are just as great today as they ever were.'
> David Rockefeller

73

what does your image say about you? It's amazing what a slight change in wardrobe can do to spruce up your appearance. Think about accessories too – I don't just mean what you put around your neck – what about the way you present your ideas? Do you have a professional looking powerpoint presentation or a few tatty OHP acetates? Do you scrounge up a scrap of paper in a meeting or do you have a leather bound folio and a spare pen? Like so much of what I am discussing, it is all about finding a balance to portray the correct image for you and what you do.

Almost by definition, most people are average and are happy to be that way.

Averageness travels likes a contagious disease – do not make yourself copy others' average bad behaviour.

You want to stand out from the crowd and not just blend in to the competition. When you are asked about what you do for a living, don't just say you are a lawyer. There are a lot of lawyers. Tell them what you bring to being a lawyer and what unique aspects of your nature and character make you the type of lawyer you are. You are a product as far as networking is concerned, and a unique selling point is important in selling any product, so celebrate the things that make you different.

Impressions are not about one thing – they are based on the whole package not the pretty wrapping paper that is comes in.

The spotlight is on you – and what you say

Of course, despite all the listening you do and how well dressed you are with just the right amount of make-up or sharp tie, sometimes people will want to hear what you have to say. This too is part of the

'The freethinking of one age is the common sense of the next.'
Matthew Arnold

image you must portray because essentially you are being judged either consciously or sub-consciously by people deciding if they can work with you or buy your product or service. There are no rules here that you don't already know; avoid politics, sex and religion as much as you possibly can.

Be positive in what you say about yourself and your product of course, but don't belittle the competition or dismiss them out of hand. If you are much better than anyone out there, let your clients find that out for themselves or work it out for themselves – don't feel you need to tell them. Another way of looking at it is: by praising the competition and saying how much you admire what they are doing, you are by reflection saying what qualities you admire and suggesting that you have them too. Compare yourself with the best and you put yourself in the same category.

Know what you want to say always so that you can be brief and to the point. Catch the attention of your audience from the beginning and leave them with the impression of someone who is committed to something they believe in and will deliver on their promises. You can say all that without actually spelling it out just by the way you talk about yourself and your product or service. Try not to complain. It's so easy to get talking about how miserable the weather is (I work in Glasgow- it can be very easy!) but far better to be talking about something positive. Someone enthusing about a film they have just seen and how wonderful the story was or how beautiful the sets in a play they attended will make a far more lasting positive impression. It hardly matters what you are talking about – it is more to do with leaving an image of a happy positive person who is enjoying life and will make people feel good to be around them.

> *'Talk of nothing but business, and dispatch that business quickly.'*
> Aldus Manutius

Are you FAB in your elevator pitch ?

One of the important things to keep in mind when you are in a networking situation is how to succinctly describe yourself. Don't be boring, but don't be long winded. Don't patronise the other person but don't be too clever or employ technical jargon.

We have all heard of the elevator pitch where you are meant to be able to sell your product to an investor/client within 30 seconds (the length of a journey in an elevator). Well I think that the elevator pitch is old-hat and is not that attractive either as you gasp for breath after your 30 second rant about you, you, you, and of course you ... yawn.

I like to think being FAB is slightly nicer. It allows you to breath at a normal rate and remain calm and collected. Speak slowly – you have a lot to say and only a short time to say it.

Being FAB gives people a different opinion of yourself without being overbearing or downright desperate.

Being FAB means that you are not selling. Networking and selling are like oil and water ... they never mix.

What you need to be able to do when asked about your product or service is to make it FAB.

Feature   A feature describes some characteristics of a product or service.

Advantage   An advantage describes how a product, or product feature, can be used to help the buyer.

Benefit   A benefit describes how a product feature or advantage meets an explicit need as expressed by the buyer.

> *'Drive thy business or it will drive thee.'*
> Benjamin Franklin

Each situation is different and if you are selling a new anti-gravity, hyperspace teleportation unit to a group of scientists, by all means use a little technical terminology, otherwise; keep it simple. Use the language that is right for the situation. Practise in the mirror.

Hi, I'm Lindsay and I'm a ... My speciality is ...
My ambition is ... I can do ... for you.

See how it looks, practise saying it simply and briefly and when you are next introduced and you won't be tongue tied or forget to mention some vital aspect of what you are selling.

Of course, all of this will tie in to what it says on the business card you will be handing them as you describe yourself, so no need to repeat what it says there. And if you get it right and capture their attention, when they later look at the card they will also remember what you said and exactly who and what you are.

Name badges

Here is a useful tip – bring your own badge to a conference or meeting. Too often you turn up at a conference to find that the badge waiting for you (when there is one waiting for you) is misspelled, or doesn't have your company name attached. It's very difficult to achieve that blend of cool, detached, dynamic yet strangely engaging entrepreneur, when your hair is sticking to the badge which is slowly unpeeling itself from your lapel. The name might be too small to read or in some inappropriate type face. So don't leave it to chance – prepare your own and bring it with you at all times.

You want your name to appear prominently and your company name alongside. If you are trying to promote a brand image, make sure that

> *There are two ways of exerting one's strength: one is pushing down, the other is pulling up.*
>
> Booker T. Washington

it is in the correct type face and perhaps with the company logo too.

On the occasions where there are no badges supplied, yours will be even more of a talking point, but even when everyone has one, it will help that yours is different. It also shows that you are confident of who you are and what you are selling.

Just one final point on this: remember to take it off when you are leaving the venue. Don't go on to meet friends and end up at a trendy nightclub where everyone will take great delight in coming over and calling you by name until it finally clicks!

Become slightly famous

By all means become completely famous, but the idea of being slightly famous is important. When we talk about 'getting your name about', it is the best possible way of making yourself memorable in a way that costs nothing and is easily sustainable. Take the opportunity to talk at rotary clubs about what you do. A speech about your chosen subject can establish just how much you know without ever boasting directly about how well you do it. Try to find out who else might want you to talk. Local colleges might be delighted to get guest speakers talking about a profession with a direct link to their students. Talk anywhere anyone will lend you a soap box. Keep up to date with the latest developments in your chosen career so that you are ready to give your opinion when called upon. If you can establish yourself as someone who firstly has an opinion to go with their expertise, and secondly is happy to give the time to discuss that opinion, you are going to get a lot of free advertising.

The ideal is to become synonymous with your chosen line of work. When people talk about lawyers in Glasgow, there are probably no

> 'It's a little like wrestling a gorilla. You don't quit when you're tired - you quit when the gorilla is tired.'
>
> Robert Strauss

more than three names that will come to mind. These people have never shied away from the limelight and will often be seen out in front of a courtroom fiercely defending their client while happily promoting their own name. Research scientists have done the same in recent years, as have journalists working in both print and radio or television. Find a niche that you can call your own and start to promote it by writing to newspapers with your opinion. Call radio programmes and challenge politicians.

There is a company called 'A Right Pair of Chancers' run by a man called Max Cruikshank, who is an authority on youth work and drugs and alcohol counselling. Watch for him; every time there is a radio discussion about the role of the police with young people in the community, or a discussion about the classification of drugs or the dangers of solvent abuse, Max will be there. If he is not invited in to the programme, he will phone in, or email or write to the newspaper. He is a passionate and completely convincing speaker and synonymous with drug and alcohol lecturing in both the workplace and in schools, colleges or youth centres. All self promotion and all free advertising – and this is something you can do too.

'In the modern world of business, it is useless to be a creative original thinker unless you can also sell what you create. Management cannot be expected to recognize a good idea unless it is presented to them by a good salesman.'
David M. Ogilvy

6

Where Do You Network?

By now, you can answer part of this question for yourself; networking can be done anywhere, any time you meet other people. When you are out walking your dog, talking to other dog owners in the park, when you are cleaning your car and you talk to your neighbours as they pass, waiting in a queue in the supermarket, or chatting to a fellow golfer in the pro shop. It's amazing how much more effective it is talking to someone who doesn't feel the pressure of a 'sales pitch'.

When someone says to you, 'so what do you do?', it's an open invitation to explain why you like doing what you do and why you are good at it. Because they are asking the question, the other person feels they have 'discovered' you for themselves and are more likely to pass on the information to others. Remember, it's not always about talking to obvious like-minded business people, but expanding your network at every opportunity. I trust you now have your 'FAB pitch' down to a fine art and you don't need to over-do it, just explain yourself and then find out a little about them.

The same thing holds true of other leisure pursuits and outside interests; talking to people at your golf club or salsa club means you don't even need to buy a dog!

> 'When it is not necessary to make a decision,
> it is necessary not to make a decision.'
> Lord Falkland (1610 - 1643)

Networking is a lot like dating in this respect; you meet someone and chat for a bit to find out what you have in common and before long you both know if there is any future in the relationship. And just like dating, you can go about it many different ways. Don't restrict yourself to downing pints or daquiris in your local – there is always online dating. With the size and scope offered by the internet you can afford to be a little choosy if you wish.

On the one hand, you may feel the benefit of talking to a specialist group of like-minded business people. There are groups dedicated to so many small niche markets that it's unlikely you will not be able to find a site with links to your own area of expertise or a group who are looking for someone like you to provide that expertise.

Networking online has other benefits; not only can you expand the possibilities to reach others around the world but with the difference in time zones, you can be effectively networking away while you sleep.

Don't forget that the rules of networking apply equally here too; just by talking to people with similar interests, you are spreading that net. So if you have a penchant for rare Cornish garden gnomes and are a member of an internet forum of like-minded souls, it's still an opportunity to explore other possibilities and meet new people.

Another possible benefit is the chance to meet and chat to people who are doing the same thing you are doing but in a different market; someone in your own line of work and in your own town or country may be reluctant to share their ideas or processes and working methods, but if you are far enough away that you don't pose a threat or provide competition, they will probably be delighted to swap experiences and ideas.

> *'I rate enthusiasm even above professional skill.'*
> Edward Appleton

This can be particularly helpful if you are working on your own and don't have any colleagues working alongside you to share your thoughts. If you are working in a large organisation, the same thing may be applicable; someone who doesn't think you are after their job can shed light on the secrets of their success or the benefit of learning from their mistakes in a way that the girl at the next desk might feel would be counter productive for them.

A lot of networking takes place at conventions and meetings dedicated to specific professions from hairdressers to management consultants, so think twice before binning that invitation to attend a two day conference. It may have more value than you imagined no matter what the quality of the speakers.

Then there are awards ceremonies; this is a great way to meet all sorts of people while raising your own profile. Not only are people relaxed and off their guard, they will be receptive to hearing about the way you run your business and what makes you good at what you do. It is well worth entering a competition or putting your company forward for an award even if you don't fancy your chances of actually taking home a trophy.

From a business perspective, it is good practice to compare yourself with the best in your field and to find out what others value in that field. But from a networking angle you often meet people in different fields who are at a similar level of development which gives you the chance to bounce ideas off each other and form strong friendships and business ties. And they are fun!

At this point, it's worth mentioning that networking doesn't have to be about work – there is no reason that you can't use your skills to improve your knowledge about your hobbies, or if you do some

'Money often costs too much.'
Ralph Waldo Emerson

charity work, it can be a vital source of information and contacts.

Remember that you must think of networking as a lifestyle choice and apply it to every important part of your life. In fact, just as a quick off the cuff example, there are networking organisations for:

chilli growers
call centre workers
running groups
photographers
online gaming
dating
food groups
golfers
music lovers
religious groups
tall people
local bands
salsa dancing
engineering
ex pats

In fact it's probably more difficult to think of a niche group that doesn't have some sort of association or support network. With the dominance and penetration of the internet, it's difficult for anyone to be too isolated in terms of their work or interests or even disability.

Networking organisations

With that thought, there are of course organisations whose sole purpose is to WD40 the wheels of the networking new-comer and support those who are already well established, and no matter where you are it should

'Every answer asks a more beautiful question.'

ee cummings

be possible to find a suitable group for your own needs.

To expand your network quickly and target people with your similar interests, it makes sense to join groups of people

Choose groups strategically

- Customer common groups – business referral groups

- Special purpose groups – venture capital/job hunting

- Business referral groups – getting business and generating referrals

- Networking organisations – including professional development courses

- Professional associations

- Industry specific organisations

- Workplace task force/committees

- Chambers of Commerce

- Civic and service organisations

- Volunteer Groups

- Hobby Groups

- Internet Groups

- Health clubs

- Alumni groups / MBA groups

'Everything comes with instructions, except human beings.'
Anon

- Religious organisations
- Children connections – i.e. your son plays in a rugby team

Examples of these groups are:

→ Entrepreneurial exchange

→ Women in Business

→ Chambers of Commerce

→ Junior Chambers of Commerce

→ BNI

→ Rotary

→ We Entrepreneurs – International

→ Princes Trust

→ West Midlands Forum

→ Shell Livewire

→ Aspire Business Network

Examples of online groups:

→ www.BNI.com

→ www.Ecademy.com

→ www.CallCentreVoice.co.uk

→ www.networkingwomen.co.uk

'If you tell the truth, you don't have to remember anything.'
Mark Twain

➜ www.scottishbusinesswomen.com

These are simply examples and it won't take you long with a computer and a search engine to come up with the groups who relate more closely to your own ambitions and interests.

Your network is unique – it will not be a carbon copy of anybody else's network. You will develop your own contacts for your own reasons

Next step for you

1. List organisations that you're involved with – long term objectives

2. Ask yourself, 'Who would I like to meet and where can I find that kind of person?'

3. I recommend that you choose one group which will contribute to:

   - your professional development

   - potential customers or clients frequent

   - cultivating associations with business

   - making you visible in your marketplace.

Networking hotspots

Personally, I love entrepreneurial exchanges because you can learn from others who are genuinely keen to share their experiences and willing to help in what is usually an informal environment – but they are also great fun and raise a lot of money for charity.

> *'There is none so blind as those who will not listen.'*
> William Slater

I also like **We Entrepreneurs** because you can sit down for dinner in a relaxed environment with other business owners.

'Our events are not only great fun – but very effective in generating new business. Our ethos to 'learn, help and create' has struck a chord with those with those who come along and has allowed us to nurture an open culture of real support. A typical we-entrepreneur is focused dynamic, progressive and a risk taker.'

Richard O'Connor, Founder of We-entrepreneurs International

Women In Business is also great because it is full of like-minded women who are all starting in business. They offer great learning opportunities by learning from others who have been in the same situation and on that extremely large learning curve.

No – don't go all huffy because you are a man and they won't let you in, there will be all sorts of groups who will be just as relevant to you, so if you stop sulking for a minute I will continue...

Friends networks

There is a danger of feeling that it's inappropriate to use your friends for business reasons or to advance your prospects but I don't subscribe to that view; real friends will be only too happy to help and if they have groups or contacts that can be of use to you will be delighted to have the opportunity to use them for you. Wouldn't you do the same for them if or when the situation was reversed? If nothing else, it's a way of knowing how good a friend you have. They might be members of a club and invite you along sometime, or carry a few of your business cards with them to distribute in strategic areas. If you explain what you are trying to achieve, the chances are they will be

> *'A mistake is a mistake if you don't learn from it.'*
> Unknown

just as enthusiastic and enjoy going 'out there' and marketing on your behalf.

School clubs/graduates

Look at all the friends and colleagues you have known in the past and who would probably, at least in most cases, be fascinated to know what you are doing now. 'Friends Reunited' is one of the biggest success stories on the internet and also one of the most surprising for many people. Who would have thought that in a world notoriously difficult to get people to part with their money – a site dedicated to finding the people we knew at school would become so huge?

Yet, isn't this the essence of the networking philosophy? And the same thing applies to graduate groups – those we struggled alongside, who knew us in the past, many of whom would be interested in what we are doing now and feel enough of a bond of mutual experience to be glad of the chance to renew the friendship and possibly help where they can.

Remember networking is all about being curious, and if you think back to all the people you knew at school and the way they were then, it would be more than interesting to find out what they are doing now and the type of person they have become.

Glass ceiling?

Is there really a glass ceiling for women in business? I was at a launch of a business magazine for women a couple of years back and there were around half a dozen speakers that evening from all walks of business life and the media. Every single person who squared up to

> '*Always do the right thing. This will gratify some people and astonish the rest.*'
> Mark Twain

the microphone that night used the expression 'glass ceiling'. There were a couple of my male friends with me that night who were both amused at this and had taken to counting the references. Personally I think that if it exists, whining about it will not change a thing and that only by getting out there and making a success of what you do regardless of gender, can you explode the myth. Women will always have an important part in any business field, every bit as important as their male counterparts so let's not make ourselves sound weak and insecure by looking for excuses in our lack of progress. Focus on your goals and don't let anyone get in your way. This is true for all of us; male, female, young or mature!

Speed networking

Like speed dating, this is not for everyone. We each have our own preferred way of assessing others and forming relationships, business or personal. But if you are the type who can tell at a glance if they like the look of someone, then this is a fantastic way of making a lot of contacts in a very small space of time. Where speed dating is a lot of single people being given a few minutes to put across their personalities and trying to make a connection, speed networking is much less stressful; any room full of business people will potentially have something to offer, so you don't need to worry about meeting your soul-mate because in this situation every contact can be of use and they won't resent you forming a relationship with someone else in the room. This is the way it works

Armed with a ream of business cards, you are given the chance to speak and listen to as many people as you can manage in a very short space of time. You swap ideas and information with one of the participants, and when that time is up, you seek out someone else, like

'Learn something about everything and everything about something.'
Thomas Hardy

finding a partner at a school disco, and off you go again. This has the advantage of stripping the job down to its bare essentials, namely telling them about you while they tell you about them. At which point you can move on and talk to the next person without fear of appearing rude.

If first impressions count, then this is the arena where that is going to matter even more than usual. Because there is such a small window of opportunity to make any impression, you won't have the chance to change someone's mind if your first impression is not a good one. So make sure that you have that 'FAB' speech clear in your head, along with all the precepts we discuss here in this book, and look on the bright side: if you do make a hash of it, you won't have to endure your mistake long before going on to try and do better next time.

Don't be too aggressive but also remember that the whole point of the exercise is networking and everyone else in the room is there for the same purpose so don't be embarrassed to talk about business and promote yourself. Of course with all that said, it's important that in a five minute conversation you give the other people a chance to tell you about themselves.

Here too is another situation where a good business card, perhaps even one with your picture on it, is vital because in the flurry of introductions and short intense conversations, it would be very easy to lose track of who was who at the end of it all. You may have met someone called Alistair who was the answer to your dreams, you remember that he was tall with fine cheek bones and piercing blue eyes not to mention a large portfolio, but was it Alistair Anderson or Alistair Gordon? Because one of the Alistairs was a pushy sales guy who you spent your time trying to escape!

So, try to make notes of who you were speaking to, perhaps jot

> *'Words are, of course, the most powerful drug used by mankind.'*
> Rudyard Kipling

something down on the back of their business cards. You don't even need to be surreptitious about it – when you ask them something about what they do, take their card and scribble a note on the back. They will assume you are writing 'interesting girl, phone soon,' even if what you are actually writing is 'there's five minutes of my life I will never get back!'

More sales bigger promotions

The very essence of this book is the concept of spreading your net far and wide, reaching as many people as possible. But every good rule has at least a caveat if not an actual exception; given the choice of spending five minutes with the procurement manager of the business you are approaching, or five minutes with the boy who takes the mail around the building, pick the former. Flippancy aside, there will be times when you must decide who is the best person to approach and you must ensure that person is a decision maker.

In every company or management structure, there are people who can make things happen and people adept at keeping their heads below the parapet and never making decisions in case they draw fire. In some cases, you can make an initial contact within a company with someone who is just too far down the pecking order and would have to defer to someone else, who would have to check with his boss,who in turn would need it passed to his superior for a signature... and so on.

Try to make your relationships count and if you must chose between two people in an office structure, go for the one who writes his or her name on the approval slip. If you reach too high and the person you speak to feels it would be better handled at a lower level, that's fine,

> 'Give your dreams all you've got and you'll be amazed at the energy that comes out of you.'
>
> William James

in most cases you will get further, faster if you go from the top down rather than climbing every step from the bottom.

A very good friend of mine decided he had a concept that would stop trains crashing and derailing but didn't know what to do next. He felt that going to the National Enterprise company would be a start but felt that were he to walk in the front door of the organisation with his drawing and a couple of pages of foolscap paper filled with his scribbles, he would be laughed back on to the street. His solution? He emailed the Managing Director of Scottish Enterprise, mentioned a couple of the executives in the organisation he knew to establish his bona fides and got a phone call within the hour from the two experts in the company. They both made time in their diaries and had a meeting with him before the week was out. (I believe that the invention was eventually found to resemble an idea already patented in the States and would have been too difficult to differentiate for registering a new patent, but at least he wasn't laughed out of the building.)

When you get a message passed down through a management structure from above, you don't ignore it, you deal with it quickly and thoroughly. If it comes from below it is easy to put it to one side and decide that you will get to it later (once you have dealt with the missives from above!)

> 'In the modern world of business, it is useless to be a creative original thinker unless you can also sell what you create. Management cannot be expected to recognize a good idea unless it is presented to them by a good salesman.'
>
> David M. Ogilvy

7

When to Network

The trick is to make this a part of what you do all the time not something you do while you are waiting for something to happen. Networking is a way of life, not just another task to put on your 'to do' list.

There are people who hide away in their offices, or work from home in a private study like some latter day Frankenstein hoping one day expect to emerge into the light with a business plan and take the world by storm. Needless to say, I don't subscribe to this way of working, and though I would stop short of chasing them down the street with a pitch fork, I despair that more people don't realise how much easier it is to work as part of a team and to seek out the help of friends and colleagues. Who knows, maybe Frankenstein's monster would have been able to integrate with society if his father had a few more social skills.

With that in mind, it pays to share your philosophy as well as your business ideas or concepts – in other words, encourage others to do what you are doing here and get out there and actively network. The funny thing is that the one thing no one ever talks about at a network meeting, is networking – the one thing they all have in common.

> *'Integrity without knowledge is weak and useless, and knowledge without integrity is dangerous and dreadful.'*
> Samual Johnson

By all means buy twenty copies of this book and distribute them among your friends – I am sure I can negotiate a discount – but that's not what I am talking about. Try to make sure that what you pass on is in turn passed on to a wider network and sometimes the only way to do that is to come right out and ask your friends, 'did you get the chance to speak to such and such?' Be pro-active and make sure that your network doesn't stagnate.

What do you talk about?

In a previous chapter on exploding the myths of networking, I mentioned that you don't have to be funny. If you are naturally funny and you are looking for work as an after dinner speaker, don't let me stop you, but for the rest of us; don't sweat it. Talk about the weather. Seriously, it has become a cliché in its own right but it's something we all know a little about. If you are a nuclear physicist and you open a conversation with a hair stylist with a comment on the latest theory on the relationship between quarks and their role in sub-atomic molecular degradation within a relativistic particle acceleration process, he or she might surprise you with some theoretical insights, but the odds are against it. If you ask them 'what do you think about the break down of the Mitchell brothers' relationships on Eastenders' you will have started a conversation.

Because that is the point of the exercise – making a start. Unless you are that Frankenstein scientist who never integrates with the rest of the outside world and your idea of a night out involves a shovel and a graveyard, you should be able to find some common ground with most people, be it pop culture, literature or a common interest in Salsa dancing.

> 'Even if you think you are on the right track, you will get run over if you just sit there.'
>
> Will Rogers

These social exchanges also reflect what I discussed on the subject of body language; it does not matter so much what you say as how you say it. Concentrate on listening and finding something interesting about the other person and they will feel interesting when they are talking to you. In turn they will enjoy speaking to you and be more receptive to what you have to tell them.

If you are getting a train to a venue, flick through the Metro, and read the sport, the gossip and the TV guide. You won't be sitting an exam but there is nothing more likely to lose you a potential contact than failing to communicate in the most perfunctory manner. If you meet someone who asks, 'Did you see Eastenders last night?' under no circumstances reply, 'I don't own a television – I was engrossed in a new literary critique of Daumier and his role as the Michaelangelo of caricature' Even if it's true!

There is nothing sneaky or underhand about complimenting a woman's hair if she has clearly gone to some trouble with her appearance. As long as what you are saying is sincere and spontaneous, it will come across that way. And remember to smile.

No matter what topic of conversation you hit on, be friendly and smile a lot.

CAP Code and legal stuff

It is well worth remembering that there are rules and guidelines that apply to all marketing literature. It's expensive enough to produce flyers and brochures in the first place without having someone coming along and telling you it breaches the rules of marketing and you will have to scrap the lot. 'CAP' is an acronym for The Committee of Advertising Practice and it is their job to regulate the claims made and

> 'The most valuable of talents is that of never using two words when one will do.'
> Samual Jefferson

ascertain if marketing communications are 'legal, decent, honest and truthful.'

The good news is that there is a CAP Copy Advice team who can help you if there is any doubt. While I am sure you wouldn't deliberately be misleading with your leaflets, it can be very easy to employ a little hyperbole when selling yourself.

In the UK, the *British Code of Advertising, Sales Promotion and Direct Marketing* is the rule book for all non-broadcast advertising. These organisations have the backing of the Department of Trade and Industry and The Office of Fair Trading. There are various websites with a lot of information to guide you.

The boundaries of 'decency' are often stretched in the 'viral marketing' campaigns that are now a weapon in the advertising arsenal of many companies big and small, but don't be tempted to try the more 'near the bone' type of approach. Remember that while people have the choice of opening an email attachment and re-distributing the emails that amuse them, those same people would not be amused at some of that humour being seen by their children if it was posted through their door.

There is also the telephone preference service, and fax and mail preference service that I would pay particular attention to if you are directly marketing to your consumers. Under Government legislation introduced on 1st May 1999 and replaced on 11th December 2003 by the *Privacy and Electronic Communications (EC Directive) Regulations 2003*, it is unlawful to make unsolicited direct marketing calls to individuals who have indicated that they do not want to receive such calls. It is also unlawful to send an individual an unsolicited sales and marketing fax without prior permission.

> *'A dream is just a dream. A goal is a dream with a plan and a deadline.'*
> Harvey Mackay

The Telephone Preference Service can also accept the registration of mobile telephone numbers. However, it is important to note that this will prevent the receipt of live marketing voice calls but not SMS (text) messages. This is because under the *Privacy and Electronic Communications (EC Directive) Regulations 2004,* it is unlawful to send an unsolicited sales and marketing text message. Telemarketing companies who wish to send SMS messages need clients' prior permission. The Information Commissioners Office (ICO) is responsible for the enforcement of these regulations. You can be fined if you call or contact someone who has expressly asked for no contact. For more information contact: **www.tpsonline.org.uk** or **www.mpsonline.org.uk**

How do I ask for help and contacts?

You are not pretending to be running a charity organisation. In fact even if you are running a charity organisation, you are not begging. You are offering a trade here either openly or implicitly. There is no reason to be circumspect or coy when you need someone's help in business – just ask. That's the secret.

People in business (or anywhere else) appreciate honesty and honesty of approach is as good a way of stating your intention as any. If you approach someone tell them about your skills or services or product and then say, 'so what can you do for me?' that might not go down so well. But we already know we are not doing that. We are entering in to an understanding that if there is something you can do for them you will be happy to and that you expect the same. So when you see that someone can supply you with a valuable business contact, for instance, just come out and ask. But say 'please'. It stands to reason that they will be even more likely to be receptive to

'Management is efficiency in climbing the ladder of success; leadership determines whether the ladder is leaning against the rioght wall.'
Stephen R Covey

your approach if you are doing something for them, but that too can be turned around; if you are openly admitting that you can use their help it will make it easier for them to come to you.

If that sounds a little back to front, think about how much easier it is to give than to receive. If someone gives you something out of the blue or pays you an unexpected compliment, it can throw you. You may be embarrassed that you didn't pay them a compliment or just not know how to take it.

By being prepared to break the deadlock and be the first to ask for help, you remove that barrier. Who knows, perhaps the favour you do in return will be a bigger one or of more value to the other person. So never be shy about asking for help, be open, in the knowledge that given the chance, you will repay the debt in full.

What to avoid and how to move on

If you take the reverse of everything that we discuss here in this book, and imagine yourself meeting that person in a networking specific environment: that's what to avoid. If you find yourself stuck with someone whose only interest is to push their own agenda, someone there to sell and not to reciprocate or share knowledge or resources, then clearly, it's time to move on. To be brutally frank, if you find yourself in a situation where you have limited time and, literally 'people to meet, places to be' and you are talking to someone who, however interesting, has nothing to offer, it's time to move on.

Value your time in these situations, value your own resource – what you are and who you are and what you have to offer – and don't get stuck in a networking cul-de-sac; recognise that you need to move on and do it.

'When you come to a roadblock, take a detour.'
Mary Kay Ash

Pretend in your mind that you have a vaccine that can cure the whole world of a vicious strain of some virulent disease – you need to get to as many people as possible for the cure to be effective and you owe it to the world to get it out there. You don't have time to talk to anyone who might slow down that process. But how do you go about moving from one to another without appearing rude and self-serving?

'Sense is not common.'

Unknown

Always be polite. First rule. No matter how dull the conversationalist or the conversation itself, no matter how much you want to talk to someone else in the room, don't simply discard the person you are with like a soggy tissue. We have all seen the type of person who can light up the room with their smile, but can turn that smile on and off like a light switch – it appears false and insincere; telling one person you really need to get on with a dour expression on your face and then spinning to 'air kiss' someone nearby with squeals of 'darling, I haven't seen you for simply ages...' would fall into that category. Instead you must thank them for their time, perhaps even suggest that you look forward to seeing them in the future (so long as they don't then say, 'How's Tuesday for you?'). Control the conversation; be firm, direct but make it clear that you are ending the conversation and are about to leave.

Where this can be awkward is where you are leaving someone on their own and going to join another group – it appears to be callous and inconsiderate. Here's a tip I got from a seminar that I find really useful in a situation where you have to say no.

Like ending a dialogue, saying 'no' to a direct request can be hard to do in many situations. The first thing is to actually say no. It's all to easy to say, 'Oh, I'm not sure I can,' and leave the door open for someone to continue to press, so make it clear that you are not going to move from that position from the start. Now, rather than abandon them to their fate, suggest an alternative and work with them. For instance if someone wants you to do a speech and for whatever reason you don't intend doing it (and why should you have to explain yourself to me?), you may start by saying, 'No, I can't speak at that event but have you considered using Lindsay Bannerman? I'm told that she is both stunningly attractive and a fine speaker and inspiring if a little too modest.' [Steady on ... Ed.]

> 'Half the game is 90 percent mental.'
>
> Unknown

You have established from the start that you are not going to be pressed in to doing something you don't want to do, but then immediately moved on to what other alternatives are available – as if to say, 'I don't want to do it, but that doesn't mean I don't care.' So if you are in this situation in a networking event and you really want to move on, try asking if they have had a chance to speak to someone else there, perhaps even offer to introduce them yourself (clearly this is not such a good idea if the person is a crashing bore and you will not be thanked for dumping them on a colleague).

There are many ways to do it and it is can be done is such a positive and helpful way that the person involved will not even be aware they are being 'handled'.

'Don't confuse being stimulating with being blunt.'
Barbara Walters

8

I'm a Celebrity

There are two types of people at a networking event – those who drain you and those who energise you; avoid the **drainers** as much as you possibly can and make sure you never suck the energy from anyone else. You know the type – they want you to listen to their problems, complain about their colleagues, lift their spirits, but don't even think about doing anything for you.

Energisers are worth their weight in gold; they are happy, positive and willing to both give and receive – even if they are not always 'up' being 'down' doesn't define them and no matter the circumstances will have time to listen to you and hear your problems, and offer support or solutions or both.

I have a business acquaintance who made a rapid rise up the career ladder after a late start and every time things started to get her down or the pressures of work were getting to her, she would phone me up and take me for a business lunch. How do I explain this without sounding callous and indifferent? Every time we met, it would take me weeks before I had the energy to face another 'session' with her. It's not that I don't care, far from it, but sometimes you need to have a conversation with someone that isn't negative, isn't depressing and

> *'Every exit is an entry somewhere else.'*
> TomStoppard

has an element of 'give and take'. Needless to say I am busy a surprising amount of the time when she calls!

Business means business

There is an obvious trap to fall into with networking and that is comfort groups. You can easily find yourself seeking out the same old people, friends and established contacts, and blethering about your personal life, their personal lives, the football, the weather and so on. This is fine for five minutes as a warm up, but it won't get you anywhere in the long run.

Think of it this way: pretend that you are being employed by yourself and that you are paying yourself £60 per hour to go out and get results for your company. Now assess your progress at an event. Are you really giving yourself value for money?

Remember it's okay to want to talk about business, everyone else at an event is, or should be, doing the same thing. Don't feel guilty for wanting to be successful, you have my permission to succeed. It's a fact that the thing that holds back most people and prevents them from reaching their true potential is fear of winning. It seems strange but it is astonishing how many people of talent and ability will get a crisis of confidence just when they most need a driving self-belief.

There are a lot of people who succeed without any great talent but have a power and drive and blind self-confidence (sometimes in the face of striking evidence of their own shortcomings) that allows them to reach their goals and ignore the obstacles along the way. If you can tap into that kind of mindset and add a little talent and/or ability, your success is assured. Being afraid to speak up and talk about business, both yours and of those around you, is a classic sign of avoidance

> 'The profit of great ideas comes when you turn them into reality.'
> Tom Hopkins

and insecurity. Better to speak of the weather than fall flat on your face in talking about a new business venture.

So don't be afraid of success and don't fear failure either; all of the great entrepreneurs accept that you can't win every time, but know that only by picking yourself up and trying again will you ensure success. Learning from our mistakes is important to our progress and while it would be nice to have everything handed to us on a plate, the truth is that most people work for what they achieve and do it with such assurance that you might be forgiven for thinking they did it without effort. This brings us back to the message of presenting yourself as someone who is positive and not bemoaning your luck and cursing the chances that you missed.

When you are speaking in these situations, try to pace yourself; better to make what you say memorable by talking slowly and clearly than to bombard the listener with a torrent of words crashing one into the other as though you are trying to convince yourself as much as the person you are addressing. A good sales person knows how to speak with a quiet authority and that is essentially what you are doing: selling yourself and your business. If you are not sure of your product or yourself, you can easily fall in to the trap of 'over-selling' and lose your audience.

Don't re-invent the wheel

This goes back to making the best use of the people you know and the contacts you have established; if there is someone out there who has already achieved the goal you are reaching for, ask their advice. If someone has reached the top of his chosen field, he will more often than not be delighted to share his secrets. It is a sincere form of

> *'Persistence is the hard work you do after you are tired*
> *of doing the hard work you already did.'*
> Newt Gingrich

flattery to ask advice. Think of the person who does the same job as you, perhaps even works in the same company, and ask yourself if you ever considered phoning him up and seeking out some of his experiences. What's the worst that can happen? If you are embarrassed to phone and ask for help, write to him. Do you think he might feel superior to you because you are admitting he knows more, has achieved more, sold more, has a bigger, flashier car? Guess what? If he has these things, he already is superior, so swallow your pride and find out how he got there and what mistakes he made along the way. What would he do differently if he were starting again?

Strengths vs weaknesses

Some people are list makers and some are not, but try this simple exercise whatever category you are in: write down two columns – one side showing what you know you are good at, where you have had success in the past, the character traits which work in your favour, geographical advantages, good looks and charm, in short, everything you can think of that you have going for you. Now in the opposing column write down what you get wrong, the mistakes you repeat, the flaws in your character and all of the things you feel might hinder your chances of success.

Just by putting them down in black and white (I'll assume you didn't use a green pen), you are already on the way to defeating your problems. If you are honest with yourself – and remember this is just for you, not to pass around and have other people's comments – then you might find some things that you knew subconsciously but had never really faced. But don't fixate on either side of the list, its value to you is as a considered and balanced breakdown of what and who you are.

'Silent gratitude isn't much use to anyone.'

GB Stein

So if, for example, you look at the negative and think, 'Yeah, it's no wonder I am such a loser,' have an equally close look at the positive side and remember what you are capable of doing, what you must acknowledge are strong reasons for your inevitable success. Of course, the opposite is also true – don't just look at your strengths and wonder why you don't have that yacht moored off St Kitts, look at the other column and wonder what might be anchoring you down.

Top tips for networking

✠ **Visit as many groups as possible that spark your interest.** Notice the tone and attitude of the group. Do the people sound supportive of one another? Does the leadership appear competent? Many groups will allow you to visit two times before joining. There are so many factors involved that it is well worth taking this extra time to assess the type of people you will be mingling with and if it is going to be an efficient use of your time. With the best will in the world, there are only so many network events that you can or even should, attend. If your whole life is taken up with a never-ending circle of this type of event, you will be left with nothing to talk about and no social life to speak of (literally).

✠ **Remember to ask open-ended questions** that encourage the other person to tell you a little about themselves and what they do for a living. Make sure that you show a proper interest in what they are saying and concentrate all your attention on them and don't be thinking of who you are going to talk to next.

✠ **Become known as a powerful resource for others.** This is another corner stone of the networking principle – if people know

> *'It's nice to be important, but it's more important to be nice.'*
> Unknown

that they can turn to you when they are looking for help and that your response will be positive, you are far more likely to get that call. You want to be involved and at the hub of new ventures where you will pick up a lot of new contacts and help establish other people in business. These seminal points in the life of any company are often when the bonds of both friendship and trust in business are formed; people have an almost sentimental regard for the 'original' colleagues who were there at the start of any venture.

Here we also have a prime example of the 'pay if forward' principle; they know that you know that they are just starting out and don't have a clue if they will be successful. That means they also know you are helping because you want to help, not because you are trying to sell them services or make money off the back of their project. Again that encourages trust. On top of all that, it is an exciting time to see a fledgling company grow and to feel you are a part of it during that time. The chances are you will be motivated by the experience and find new energy for your own enterprises.

⊠ **Networking within your own company is a career-smart move**. Use all these skills all the time, and use them in your company for communicating with those above you in the chain of command and the people who will help you do your job and make a successful future possible.

⊠ **Be accountable to yourself for the choices you make** and for the consequences of your actions. Just as we discussed the importance of giving the best advice you can when recommending someone else in a networking situation, you must live by your decisions. We all make mistakes, and everyone

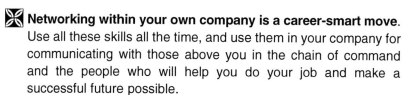

'Change is not merely necessary to life - it is life.'
Alvin Toffler

knows that, so don't pretend to be infallible – if you get it wrong hold your hands up and apologise.

⊠ **Be your own most critical critic.** Others will flatter you or avoid telling you the truth as they see it because they don't want to hurt your feelings or because they don't have the confidence to speak to you. So, if you are hard on yourself and honest (which includes being aware of doing things well and giving yourself a pat on the back) then you will learn from your own mistakes, something we all talk about but too few actually do.

⊠ **Look for opportunity.** If you are not listening, a lot of chances will pass you by. People don't always come out with a direct offer, they will often try to get a feel for your opinion or likely availability, and if you miss that type of message it can pass you by. With the best will in the world, people will just not be aware that you are in a position to help, so by listening to both what they are saying and picking up on what they are not saying and all the while reading between the lines, you will learn a lot. If that all sounds a little challenging, it is. That's why you should try speaking 20% of the time and listening for the other 79%. (I thought I would give you a spare 1% for scratching your nose – don't say I am not considerate.)

⊠ **Say, 'Thank You'.** Not only do people like their efforts to be acknowledged but they are guaranteed to notice when you don't thank them. It only takes a second but the good feeling that it engenders from the recipient (especially weighed against the negative reaction if you don't do it) means that you should never ever forget to thank someone for even the smallest of favours. You ask a waitress in any restaurant and they will be able to tell you every table where the diners have the manners to notice them

'The golden rule is that there are no golden rules.'
George Bernard Shaw

and say 'thank you' when their meals are served or the menus handed to them. And if you think you don't need to say 'thank you' to someone whose wages you are paying by patronising their restaurant, you have not been paying any attention to a thing I have written here. A close friend of mine has a twelve-year old son, Thomas, (with more attitude than is strictly good for him) who when holding a door for an adult in a shopping centre watched the man sail past without a word. Without hesitation, he sang out at his back (loudly) 'You're welcome!' To the man's credit he turned, grinned a little sheepishly and apologised. Remember there is no one you should consider below you when it comes to good manners, and when it is second nature, you will not be caught out by forgetting to thank someone.

❖ Don't wait until you need something – you must first give. The getting comes second.

❖ Don't forget the 'pay it forward' concept. If you get a chance to help someone, don't factor in how much they have done for you. We would never get very far if we waited for everyone else to do something for us before we were prepared to lift a hand for others. I believe in this principle so strongly that it is at the heart of my whole approach to networking.

❖ Always carry and use business cards, and if you don't have any, then get some. Don't say, 'Oh, I'm waiting for my cards to come from the printer,' or 'I don't have any on me.' Unless you are in the swimming pool, there is no excuse for not having a card with you, so make sure that every suit, handbag or whatever you will be wearing, has a ready supply - and distribute them liberally.

'It is a beautiful world - consciously put some little bits of it into your memory every day.'

James Alexander

9

List of Networking Organisations and Contact Details

Networking Women	www.networkingwomen.co.uk
International Business Owners	www.we-entrepreneurs.com
Womans Financial Adviser Group	www.wfa-group.co.uk
Bacon, Eggs and Entrepreneurs	www.businessbee.co.uk
Ecademy	www.ecademy.com
Call Centre Issues	www.callcentrevoice.com
Chartered Institute of Marketing (Technical)	www.cimtech.org
BNI Europe	www.bni-europe.com
Business Referral Exchange	www.brenet.co.uk
Women In Business	www.womeninbusinessnetwork.org.ul
Friends Reunited	www.friendsreunited.com
Business Link	www.businesslink.gov.uk
Virtual Networking	www.the-grapevine.co.uk
British Chambers of Commerce	www.chamberonline.co.uk
World Chambers of Commerce	www.worldchambers.com
Junior Chamber of Commerce	www.jciscotland.org.uk
Shell Livewire	www.shell-livewire.org
Princes Trust	www.princes-trust.org.uk
Everywoman	www.everywoman.co.uk
Aurora Womans Network	www.busygirl.co.uk
The Womans Company	www.thewomenscompany.com
Womans Business Network	www.wbn.org.uk
Linked In	www.linkedin.com
Rvze	www.rvze.com